I'M HUMAN—
THANK GOD!

DR. ROBERT M. McMILLAN

[signature: Rby M McMillan, Psal 23]

EDUCATION SERVICES CONSORTIUM, INC.
Tallahassee, FL

Published by Education Services Consortium, Inc., Tallahassee, Florida

Copyright © 2008 Education Services Consortium, Inc.

Cover design and text formatting done by Sarah Snyder

ISBN: 978-0-9802441-0-6
Library of Congress Cataloging in Publication Date
McMillan, Robert M.
        I'm human—Thank God!
        1. Christian life—Baptist author. I. Title.
BU 4501. 2. M275   248'.48'61   73-8813

I dedicate this new printing of "I'm Human—Thank God!" to my wife, Jeannie McMillan. It would be impossible for me to say enough about the work she has put into this manuscript, and as co-laborer with me these last 64 years in the sharing of Christ's Gospel.

Contents

Preface

In October of 2007, I learned that Dr. McMillan's book, "I'm Human--Thank God!" is out-of-print and no longer commercially available to the public. This book, published in 1973, means a great deal to me and to many other Christians; especially those of us who struggle to understand our personal challenges and human inadequacies in living a worthy Christian life. For many of us," I'm Human--Thank God!" provides positive encouragement and direction for our lives as Christians. The problem is that only a few copies of the original book are available from a limited number of owners, a few of whom are willing to share their personal copies through internet book sales; but that is not availability needed to impact a larger public.

I decided to contact Dr. McMillan about this matter to see if he would be interested in an exact reprinting of the original version of his book. A telephone conversation with Dr. McMillan and a follow up luncheon with him and his wife, Jeannie, provided an opportunity to propose to them that we put the book back into circulation. We each agreed that the message of the book and its purpose is as valid today as it was in 1973. I suggested that by preparing a new printing of the original book, not a revision or new version, we could ease the pressure that would occur with a long term re-writing effort. I also suggested that with the approval of the Board of Trustees of Education Services Consortium, Inc. (ESC Inc), funding for the project could be provided on a modified cost-recovery basis. That action would be consistent with the charter and mission of ESC Inc, a not-for-profit operating foundation chartered in 1973 through the state of Florida by myself and three other faculty members at Florida State University.

The McMillans were very excited about this unexpected opportunity to have the book reprinted and into circulation; thus resurrecting its potential as Dr. McMillan's testimony to God's grace, God's abiding love and understanding of mankind, and especially God's intent to create through the Holy Spirit an ongoing personal relationship with each individual Christian.

These first steps were the beginning point for many decisions and collaborative actions that lay ahead. The many aspects of the work have now reached fruition in this new printing of "I'm Human--Thank God!"

The greatest blessing of this endeavor for me personally has been the privilege of getting to know and revere Robert and Jeannie McMillan. Married for 64 years, and serving all those years at the pastoral level in numerous churches and several countries, they are a wonderful couple, a powerful gospel team and a marvelous witness to the love of God and the Grace of His Son.

It is an honor for Education Services Consortium, Inc. to serve as the publisher of "I'm Human--Thank God!" a book to enjoy.

Dr. William R. Snyder, President

Foreword

During sixty-four years of pastoral ministry one becomes exposed to almost every area of human need and weakness.

The sympathetic pastor soon discovers that the great majority of people become frustrated by their failures. It is not that these failures are "large" immoralities but rather the cumulative force of multitudes of minor human infractions of a popularly conceived holiness.

People desire some kind of relationship with God because of an innate need. However, they easily become frustrated at the seeming impossibility of such an experience. For very normal humans, religion can become a constant stimulus to guilt and negative thinking because of their sense of inadequacy and unworthiness.

Unrealistic goals and beliefs together with the exploitation of their emotions by certain brands of preaching have driven multitudes of good people from the churches and yet even their absence becomes a source of guilt to them.

It is evidently the desire of God that men be free of these anxieties. "Whom the Son sets free is free indeed."

In the following pages I have endeavored to emphasize the possibility of a warm relationship with God compatible with the realities of our humanity.

ROBERT M. MCMILLAN
Tallahassee, Florida

CHAPTER 1

You Happen To Be Human

By a very normal spiritual longing, Christians very often make it difficult for themselves to live with their humanity. They accept a concept of the spiritual that is too idealistic and unreal. In this way they create a mental frustration which robs them of their Christian joy. Pessimism, discontentment with themselves, fears of past and the future are all by-products of this unhappy condition.

Unrealistic attitudes and goals also aggravate hypocrisy and ultimately drive away many who really want a genuine relationship with God but who simply cannot live with the tensions created by unrealistic standards.

Jesus once warned that the children of the world have more wisdom than the children of light and it seems to me that this is one of the areas in which his observation is true. The world at large has no delusions about its humanity! Unfortunately there are too many Christians programmed by certain types of popular preaching who try to ignore their humanness or else come to believe that conversion means "dehumanizing." These necessarily live with hypocrisy, guilts, and frustrations but keep on playing the unhappy game of church. It is a bore!

I'M HUMAN—THANK GOD!

The English Bible Scholar, Dr. Martin Lloyd Jones, in his book on "Spiritual Depression" says: "There are some people who seem to think that it is wrong for a Christian ever to use common sense. They seem to think that they must always do everything in an exclusively spiritual manner. Now that seems to me to be very unscriptural" (p. 82). Dr. Jones is certainly putting his finger on the subject matter that is to confront us.

Paul Tillich also had something to say about this kind of tension inherent in our humanity when he said that, "Whenever the ideal is held against the real, truth against error, good against evil, a distortion of essential being is presupposed" (*Systematic Theology*, p. 190). Tillich would not like the word, but distortion is sin in the nature of all of us.

It would do us all good to remember that nearly all scripture is directed toward our humanity and consistently portrays the love of God in action endeavoring to harmonize humanness with Himself. The action comes from God toward man. This is fundamental to every relationship which man can have with God. Ultimately God must come to man. God keeps coming to us in spite of our humanity. He never comes to make gods of us for He knows the impossibility of that matter!

From first appearances a too lofty religious idealism may look commendable but in actual fact it is a cruel unreality. One of the greatest dangers of this kind of religious idealism is that it produces cynicism. We must recognize once and for all that God is God and that there is absolutely no way men can ever be like Him. When one thinks of the story of the Garden of Eden it is surely evident that this was the problem of the temptation.

YOU HAPPEN TO BE HUMAN

It was Satan who tempted man with the idea he could become as gods. Adam and Eve had a good try at it and discovered for the rest of us that it simply does not work. You will recall that it was God who tried to stop them in the endeavor but they refused to listen.

It seems rather pathetic to encounter Christian leaders censoriously demanding the deifying of humanity in the life of believers in an endeavor to create "spirituality," religious emotionalism or, at the very lowest, pessimistic reactions that are mentally unhealthy and dangerous.

There can be nothing more absurd and damaging than to place a human, even one regenerated, next to God in Christ and proceed to whip him verbally for not being like Jesus. The Apostle Paul was a lot more realistic about these things, for, rather than exhorting his congregations to be like Jesus, he more wisely exhorted them to be like himself. "Wherefore, I beseech you be followers of me" (I Cor. 4:16). Following Jesus is one matter but to be persistently miserable for not being like Him is absurd unless we really do believe the devil that we can be as gods. Jesus is God manifested in the flesh. He is unique and in a class all by Himself.

Karl Barth once wrote in criticism of those who spoke of identification with the Christ because he felt that the ultimate logic of their position was that men would become gods. I think that even he, however, missed a very important point in his criticism by not observing that the wonder of the gospel is not that men become gods but that God did become man. From the scriptural point of view it is God who identifies with man in the incarnation and never man identifying with God by any

3

process of deification. Jesus did not save us out of our humanity but in it.

We, too realize that there has always been a frustration created by those who preach the doctrine of justification by faith and yet resort to unrealistic legalism. Emil Brunner in his book, *God and Man*, wrote, "Since the days of the Apostle Paul the charge has repeatedly been made that the preaching of justification by faith alone and not by works paralyzes the moral will and makes men idle and careless" (p. 70).

At the other end of the scale there are some who see the human born with no intrinsic human qualities whatsoever. He is like a clean sheet of paper on which his particular society will write its rules and thus conform him to its own standards. It is supposed that his true happiness will be related to his conformity of their rules. This is the point of view in the book, *Beyond Freedom and Dignity*, by B. F. Skinner. This is also the unwitting philosophy of certain kinds of legalistic preaching among evangelicals. They, too, believe man can have a genuine experience with God only if they can burden him down with so-called Christian environmental and cultural legalisms. In the measure that he conforms to these rules he is classified as spiritual.

God recognizes the intrinsic worth of a human. It is the human who brings to the environment himself and what he is for better or for worse.

If we are only what we are by environment and training, then it might be possible to isolate certain humans from society for specialized tasks even as Plato suggested in his *Republic*. This in fact is the thesis of B. F. Skinner in his *Beyond Freedom and Dignity*. I am sure that it was not intended to be so but this is also the point of view of the separatists in evangelical churches. It is an admission that man has no intrinsic nature. The Bible contradicts this point of view. Man is biologically as well as culturally developed.

When we come to the subject of the new birth we meet the same problem. Too many Christian communities simply do not believe that anything intrinsic happens to a person when he accepts Jesus Christ as Saviour. They think that the new Christian has merely made a verbal commitment to a creed and is like a blank sheet of paper for every local preacher and teacher to write on, duplicating his own idiosyncrasies. This makes slaves of would-be believers and perpetuates fears and unrealistic goals that produce frustrations that beset too many Christians.

Rabb Joshua Loth Lebman in his book, *Peace of Mind* says,

> Take for example, our sentimental misconceptions about the chubby little gurgler in his crib. How innocent, how positively angelic, he appears as he coos engagingly under his mother's doting gaze. A little bundle of heaven he seems, and we vie with one another in ascribing the purest of emotions. But actually the chubby little darling has been revealed by modern psychology to be a bundle of powerful drives—a part of possessive love—powerful inner-rage—deep fears. If this be a fairly accurate psychograph of an infant—how then shall we picture the awful complexities of the soul that has left the crib and nursery and has entered the arena of adolescence and adult life?

I'M HUMAN—THANK GOD

Humanness is unavoidable nor will the experience of salvation really alter the basic personality traits in terms of temperament. James and John still remained "sons of thunder" while living with Jesus! Even after the day of Pentecost which some of our contemporaries promote as the end-all of spirituality, Peter was still impulsive and had to be withstood to his face by Paul for his sheer hypocrisy!

Paul in Romans, chapter 7, is being honest about his humanity when he says, "But I see another law in my members, warring against the law of my mind, and bringing my into captivity to the law of sin which is in my members . . . so then with the mind I myself serve the law of God; but with the flesh (human nature) the law of sin." There are some of course who doubt Paul's conversion in this chapter but it seems to me that this is only part of the problem. Too many Christians simply must have their apostles without sin! For some, if a character is in the Bible he has to be without sin in spite of the known facts. Paul in II Corinthians still admits that he has "fears within." Of course he also knows that, "God hath not given us the spirit of fear . . ." Apparently Paul has learned that what God originates and what man feels are unfortunately not always in agreement, otherwise there would be no need of revelation nor for that matter salvation or cleansing of sin for believers.

Whatever it is that God sees in us is known only to Him. We appear to have more violent reactions to ourselves than He does. I think Jesus illustrates this when He meets the woman at Sychar. The disciples have to be dispatched to shop so that God in Christ can deal with this women's humanness. Jesus feels no embarrassment in the encounter whatsoever but evidently the disciples on their return had large question marks in their eyes when they found Jesus talking to a woman who had so many strikes against her. She was first of all not a Jew, and secondly she was a woman of the street. Her human problem was great, but the tenderness of Jesus dealing with her remains as a revelation of the love of God.

The human problem is real enough before and after salvation without further aggravating it by unrealistic positions. We had all better realize that what we are before God will always be by the grace of imputation. Even Paul had learned that for any man to stand before God he must be ". . . found in Him not having mine own righteousness . . . but that which is through the faith of Christ . . ."

We are deeply aware that there are those whose superficial reply to this kind of presentation is, "Well, I guess we can do what we like." The answer to that is quite simple and it is that most believers do what they like in any case even when it does not agree with their creed! Besides, Paul considers this a cheap statement and answers it with the curt brevity it deserves in Romans 6, verses 1 and 2.

If we can learn to be honest about our humanness instead of talking abstract, mystical, spiritualized ambiguity about the Christian life we shall find the true joy and peace we crave and we shall remove the haunting guilts that are weakening our witness as well as that of the whole Church.

CHAPTER 2

Conduct of the New Life

"And behold, a certain lawyer stood up and tempted Jesus, saying, Master, what shall I do to inherit eternal life? And he said unto him, What is written in the law? and how do you read it? And he answering said, to Jesus, Thou shalt love the Lord thy God with all they heart, and with all thy soul, and with all thy strength, and with all thy mind; and thy neighbor as thyself. And Jesus said to him, You have answered right; do this, and you shall live. But he, willing to justify himself, said to Jesus, And who is my neighbor?" (Luke 10:25ff).

There are eternal principals whether they are in the Old or New Covenants. So often when I am having discussions with Christians and I quote a verse from the Old Testament they will say, "But that is the Old Testament," as if the Old Testament were inferior to the New. In practice many don't really accept the Old Testament as inspired. All scripture is the revelation of God, whether the Old or the New Testament. We must not break it into categories whereby we decide by our own value judgments which is more inspired than the other.

I'M HUMAN—THANK GOD

When this lawyer came to Jesus, he asked the way to eternal life. He was speaking of "life of the ages," a common Judaistic phrase.

The word life—there are several Greek words translated "life" in the New Testament—means muscular activity: living reality. It is not an abstract thing. It is not an ephemeral thing. It is not a philosophy.

When the New Testament speaks of eternal life, it speaks of activity, of action, and not at all in a mystical sense. In John 3:16, everlasting life is this kind of life. Throughout the New Testament it is consistently this type of life. It does not mean that we die then live in some kind of ghostly existence. Most of us do not really care for that concept! We do not relish the kind of eternity when we are ghosts. Eternal life is consistently, in the New Testament, real living, the kind of thing we crave.

Paul teaches that spirits have no longing to be "unclothed." So believers yearn to be "clothed upon with that which is from above." Eternal life means life that goes on through the ages, a never dying thing, a never dying experience.

The man was right, eternal life is something we obtain. His concept was not merely the going on of existence, however, but rather how do we continue to exist forever in a right relationship to God?

How can we have the continuation of life in a right, happy, wholesome relationship with God? This is the kind of life we desire to continue; the kind of life that is in harmony with God. This is heaven.

What does the law and the prophets have to say about the subject? The lawyer quotes Leviticus 19, and verse

18, when he says, "Thou shalt love the Lord thy God with all thy heart, all thy soul, all thy strength, all thy mind, and thy neighbor as thyself." Jesus agreed that this was a formula for a continued, happy relationship, forever, with God. "Go out and do it, and you will live," Jesus encouraged.

This is where the problem really begins. Evidently the man did not have the capacity to do it and the evidence is in the very next verse when he asks, "Who is my neighbor?" This is where legalism breaks down.

Jesus seems to be saying that if men could perfectly live the revealed law of God they would not need to be born again. That may be a shocking statement but it is there. When the rich young ruler of the synagogue came to Jesus and asked the same question, "Good Lord what must I do to have eternal life?" Jesus answered, "Do the commandments." The young man said, "I try to keep them all, but there is something missing in my life." He was saying, "I have tried." He had kept the Jewish practice of religion, but he knew that he had not met the standard. This is the problem with all kinds of law.

We are aware that this is a Judaistic approach to the matter. Alienation from God is a matter of natural fault rather than particular errors.

The last is like a line scale. At one end of the scale is the point of perfection, at the other end total evil. We are all some place between these points on the scale in terms of actual conduct as a confirming point of our sinful nature. Some of us may be at one point on the scale and others may be higher, but no matter where we are, we are all short of the point of perfection. We have not made it!

I'M HUMAN—THANK GOD

The man who is missing the point of perfection by a small margin is as bad as the man who is missing it by a greater margin! Neither has made it! This is one shade of the meaning of "For all have sinned and come short of the glory of God." This is why Paul declares there is no difference among people. If it is little, or much, by which we come short, we still come short.

A few years ago we were spending a vacation in Missouri at the Lake of the Ozarks. We had been water skiing and as we were coming in toward the dock we all had to get out of the boat and swim. At that, I am no great artist. I can make it for a short distance and then I give out. My wife is a good swimmer and one of our deacons who was with us is also a swimmer.

We all started off in great style. For the first few strokes, I was as good as anyone but, as we came closer to the dock, I became weaker and weaker and fell farther and farther behind. The other two were already safe on the dock. I began to think I would drown and I must have panicked. If you know how deep the Lake of the Ozarks is you would know how I felt. They were on the dock and did not fully realize I was in real difficulty. I could hear them calling, "It's not far, it's not far. Come on. Just a few more feet." And it was. But whether I was only a few feet or twenty feet from that dock, the same amount of water would have drowned me! You see, the few more feet was very poor consolation to a man who was in a panic and exhausted!

The thing I am trying to say by illustration is that Jesus realized that if a man were capable of keeping all the revelation of the law given by God, he would not need to be born again for he would have no sins to be atoned for. He would be perfect. But we cannot do it. This is why the Word became flesh and dwelt among us. The spoken and written word was insufficient. It had to be put into fleshly form to become man like we are and dwell in our circumstances in order to save us.

Going back to my illustration, somebody on the dock telling me that it is only a few more feet is of absolutely no value to me. But that could be exactly the legalistic picture of God in relationship to me. He could be standing in the security of the eternal dock saying to humankind, "It is only a few more feet," but that is of no value to exhausted, frustrated, drowning men.

We can drown under good advice, even the spiritually good advice of the law of God. If God really wants to do something about it, He must get off the dock and get into the water beside us. He must have the capacity not only to conquer the element of danger but to know enough about what He is doing to take us safely home when we cannot do it ourselves. Now there is the miracle of the gospel.

The law is like God standing on the dock, but when the Word becomes flesh and dwells among us, it is God in Christ getting into our circumstance. He gets into our dilemma, our problem, our anxiety, out weakness, our frustration with this difference. He knows how to handle it. He knows how to conquer it. He knows how to beat it and He did it and, therefore, has shown his capability to take us safely ashore. Therefore, we must rest confidently in Him and not struggle. This is the difference between law and grace.

Now let us look at the real possibility of Jesus'

statement in this context. Having been born of the Spirit of God, we are indwelt by capacities by which we can now do what God requires of us. We can have the capacity, in Him and because of Him, to live. Whereas prior to redemption and the indwelling of his Spirit we tried alone and failed, He now is in our circumstance with us. This is the wonder of it all. He is in our circumstance and helps us in our circumstance. And so the statement becomes true, "to love the Lord thy God with all thy heart, all thy soul, all thy strength, all thy mind, and your neighbor as yourself." It really only becomes practical after the re-birth.

LOVE THE LORD WITH ALL THY HEART

The heart of the bible is the psychological center.

Figuratively this is true, it is not an actual fact. The heart is not literally the seat of the emotions but in the Bible people said it as they felt it. The Bible expresses emotions in terms of the visceral. The bible describes our yearning after someone "with the bowels of compassion." Actually what it means is with the stomach. Our stomach has a physical reaction to our emotion! We still use this kind of language. I have heard them singing about "chills run up and down my spine." This is the same type of statement.

When the heart pumps a little faster we feel it, and it becomes a description of the emotions when a young fellow sees a young girl and he thinks this is the one, his heart begins pounding! We can understand then why we say, "I love you with all my heart."

When the Bible exhorts us to love the Lord God

with all our heart, it implies a felt thing. We feel it! I don't quite agree with people who say that we don't have to feel the Gospel. We don't have to feel saved, that is true, but if we are saved, we feel it. There is emotion. If there is no emotion, there is little love. So Jesus said this is how we are to love God.

This heart relationship with God is not to be a philosophy to which we subscribe. It is something that will make our hearts beat a little faster. It will get us excited. I think too much of this has been lost to us.

Some years ago someone conceived the cultural stupidity that it is something less than normal to express emotion in religious matters. They did it in Britain where I grew up. Churches became so cold, frigid, precise, grammatically and theologically correct that it was like going into a refrigerator.

Dr. Stanley Jones in the *Christ of the Indian Road* described this sad state when he described a service as "Faultily faultless, icily cold and splendidly null."

We must not be afraid to love the Lord our God with all our heart! I am glad the Bible puts it in this sequence. First of all, "Love the Lord thy God with all thy heart."

"Love the Lord thy God with all thy soul," is the second step of this practical progression.

This is spiritual. This goes deeper. We can be emotional but there are times when a deep trust, a peace and a restfulness comes over us and it is not the time for emotional reaction. It is the time for complete subjection of the spirit till the heaviness of peace overwhelms us. This is reaching down a lot deeper than emotion. It is reaching into the very soul and being, and it is a happy link and relationship with God.

I'M HUMAN—THANK GOD

This is the spiritual aspect of it.

LOVE THE LORD THY GOD
WITH ALL YOUR STRENGTH

This is physical. Jesus is weaving a pattern that is the whole gospel for the whole man. Get the emotion. But we have people who want to live with the emotion all the time. This is as abnormal as none at all. There are people who are seeking religious emotional "kicks." Emotions are there for a significant, essential and an important contribution to our total life but it is equally important that we possess a tranquility of relationship that is spiritual. It is also important that even this progresses until it becomes action and conduct.

When we were just married, we went to our first little church. It was during war-time rationing and we were allowed two sausages and two eggs a week which we always kept until after church on Sunday night. We felt that was the time that we could most relax. I had a friend with whom I had been in college and he had not yet gotten into a pastorate and was working as a colporteur. He came to our village selling Bibles for the Bible society. He did not bring and ration books with him! We shared our sausages and eggs with him, and two eggs and two sausages had to go three ways that week!

After we had our little repast, if you could call it that, we sat at the fireplace and began to talk about old times and theological problems. My wife was meantime doing the dishes. Presently, the dishes began getting louder and louder, until I received the impression she was trying to tell me something!

I left my friend for a moment and went back to the sink, and it didn't take me long to learn there was something seriously wrong and I had not known it. I put my arm around her and said, "Darling, I love you." She just turned to me and said, "If you love me, do something. Dry the dishes." She had just about had enough, you see.

It was an important message and a new experience for me for it introduced the dimension of work and action into our love relationship! Sure it was nice and warm to say, "I love you honey." Any fool can say that. But to let it proceed from emotion into the depth of the spirit and then into physical action and strength, makes it a lot more genuine.

Love is not merely emotion, it is not merely spiritual intimacy, it is the cumulative force of all of these things translated into action. So a true love for God demands conduct. Agape, love, is total commitment of the person.

LOVE THE LORD WITH ALL YOUR MIND

"Love thy Lord God with all thy heart (emotions); thy soul (spiritual); thy strength (physical); and now, lastly, with all your mind (intellectually)." This is something we neglect too much, as Christians. The development of our minds is very important to our eternal life. This is significant for the going on of life. The Bible shows, I believe, that the continuance of my being in relationship to God will rise no higher than what I am when I go to be with the Lord. In other words, if your mind is a dried-out place with nothing to fall back on and no resources, do not expect, when you get to heaven to suddenly become a Ph.D., by the act of God! The Ph.D.'s around know that would be a cheat?

When the Bible speaks about rewards in heaven, some have the rather simplistic concept that God has a large table of big trophies made of gold and worth a lot! Maybe they can have a $10,000 reward if they are good! Rewards to these light up the eyes. When one reads the New Testament, the reward is in the context of the Olympic games. You know what the reward was? The laurel wreath! Worth about a dime!

We need to learn that the nurture of our total life now, including our minds, is imperative to the continuance of our experience at journey's end. The learning process does not end, nor are the years of mental assimilation wiped out. Eternal life continues these as part of the bliss of heaven. When Jesus says, "well done," it is the reward of our accomplishments including the development of our minds. There are evidently degrees of bliss in heaven. Every believer should develop and nurture his mind because he loves God.

God can only use what is available in any one of us. The more we equip ourselves, the more He has to work with. Brains were his original idea and nowhere in time nor eternity has God renounced their necessity or worth.

So legalism carried to its logical conclusion can only be satisfied by perfection. But such is not the nature of man. However, the new nature in man received through Christ makes conduct a meaningful possibility through spiritual growth and development.

CHAPTER 3

Does God Accept Our Humanity

Peter is a real favorite Bible character. Oh, they are all good, but I like Peter. I think I like Peter because of his humanness. I often think of him being like the beloved and proverbial Irishman who every time he opens his mouth, "puts his foot in it!" There is something appealing about the naturalness of Peter. In John 21, verse 15, the Lord, after his resurrection, met with Peter and asked, "Peter, do you love me more than these?"

Do you love me? This is also the question of our day. Wherever we go, we see young people with signs of one kind or another, either on their automobiles or on their shirts, telling us the news that they want more love. We are not certain what they mean by the word "love". when they use it in their context!

It is interesting that Jesus when He meets Peter does not ask, "Do you believe in me?" He does not ask, "What are your theological opinions concerning me?" He does ask, "Do you love me?" The Bible is an honest book. It has been criticized and analyzed; it has been taken apart yet it is still with us. Everyone ought to agree that it is honest in its vision of humankind. The Bible does not expect too much from men. It promises, however, to do much for them! The Bible does not begin with impossible demands of us; it attempts to do the impossible for us. The Bible does not isolate heaven from us; it brings heaven to us. The Bible does not put God in the distance of space; the Bible brings God to earth to dwell among us, to be tempted in all of his faculties as we are, and yet be without sin. Yet in the midst of it all, it looks at men as they are!

If we are to understand this encounter Peter had with Jesus, we must understand the background. We must get to know Peter. Allow me to hurriedly give you a sketch of Peter. Just in case you think I am adding things, I want to assure you that everything I say about Peter is supported from the Scripture. So often people idealize Bible characters making them what they are not.

Out of honesty, Peter does not belong on a stained glass window. He simple does not fit! He belongs beside each of us. Let us think about him for a moment and as we do, use his person and character as a mirror for our own humanity.

Peter was the first disciple, together with his brother Andrew, to be called to follow Jesus (Mark 1) . That seems a very innocent statement, doesn't it? But when humans get involved in firsts, the simple becomes very complex. Peter immediately and from that day on assumed he was first! He talked first, acted first, and assumed leadership that was not given to him by anyone. It was presumptuous leadership.

We all think we are special. I too think I am quite distinctive! We like to say, "I am the first." People love to tell us, "I was the first one to come into the new sanctuary." "When they opened the doors of the church, I was the first one in." "I was the first to do this." "I was the first to do that." It gives us a sense of priority. We all have the desire to rise above our fellow humans, and with this ego of ours, to be distinctive, unique and apart from the crowd. Peter was precisely like this. A very normal human reaction.

Jesus called Peter first! Forget about his brother, Peter was first! From then on he was usually the first to talk, even if he talked nonsense as he did on occasions! But being first, we humans feel we have right, we have authority.

Peter was also a religious experimenter. Most humans are. We like to play with or at religion. Do you recall that experience when Jesus sent the disciples in the boat so that he could go and get a little rest from them? Apparently, even the Lord has to get a change from disciples now and again! The Lord went to a mountain to pray and instructed the disciples to go in a boat to the other side of the lake where he would meet them later. The story is in Matthew 14.

A storm arose and those experienced fishermen, Peter, James and John were afraid. It must have been quite a boat for all of them to be in it. Twelve of them at least. The seas became tempestuous and the winds blew until the disciples were scared to death of what might happen to them. We are told that, in the middle of the night (in the fourth watch), someone came walking on the water. The Bible declares that the disciples were scared out of their wits. So would you! And then one said to the other, "It looks like Jesus." Peter felt it was a ghost, but if it was Jesus, he was going to find out. Here is our religious experimenter! In a flash, the laws of gravity notwithstanding, Peter was over the side of the boat and on the water! Of course one can't last very long, as a human, doing this kind of thing without sinking. Peter began to sink, and then cried to Jesus to save him. Jesus saved him and took him into the ship.

This is Peter. This is human! He is not content to believe Jesus for who he is. He is not content to believe Jesus for the power and authority of his words. It is always the weak in faith who need to walk on the water especially when there is no good reason for doing it except religious experimenting. It would have been so much more comfortable and wise to stay in the boat! The Lord was still going to perform the greatest miracle of them all and still the storm.

Weak faith in all of us keeps looking for the miraculous, the special. Some think it a sign of higher spirituality the more we become involved in miracles. In fact, the Lord tells us that miracles required by people in order to buoy their faith is a sign of the weak and not the strong. It is more difficult to stay in the boat sometimes when the storm is raging! It is more difficult to ride out the storms of life without having any great miracle happen to us and be content until the Lord comes in his time and in his way to still the storm. But Peter was a religious experimenter.

We have all asked God for what now appears to be ridiculous miracles in our lives. This is part of our growing up experience. As we look back I am sure we are thankful God did not do anything about some of those requests!

One day the disciples were standing together when Jesus asked them what men were saying about Him. The disciples replied that some people thought he was John the Baptist come back again while others thought he was Elijah, the prophet forecast to come back again. But Jesus said, "Who do you say that I am?" The man who answered was Peter! He said, "Thou art the Messiah, the Son of the living God."

For once Peter was right. Jesus said, "Blessed are you Simon, son of Jonah." The next phrase gives us Jesus' view of Peter's character. He knew that if he did not do something to humble Peter, getting the right answer would have made him absolutely and utterly unbearable to live with! So Jesus said to him, "Peter, flesh and blood have not revealed this to you. You did not think this out for yourself, Peter, but my Father, who is in heaven, came in a ministry of the Holy Spirit and revealed it to you! I am the Messiah, I am the Son of the living God and on this great confession, I will build my church."

Paul confirms this statement in Romans 10, verse 9: "That if thou shalt confess with thy mouth the Lord Jesus, and believe in thine heart that God has raised him from the dead, thou shalt be saved." This is the rock on which Christ has built the Church, and the gates of hell cannot prevail against the security of the believer who has known, through the Holy Spirit, who Jesus is.

We must learn that if we are to know Jesus it will not come by intellectual or logical deduction, but when the Holy Spirit quickens us in our hearts and minds and opens our spiritual eyes to see in Jesus not a mere man of history, but God come into our perplexity to save us from our sins. When this happens, we must remind ourselves that we did not come to the experience by any cleverness, but only because God, the Holy Spirit, came to us.

Do you recall the story of the Mount of the

Transfiguration? That was quite a day, was it not? Peter, James and John went up the Mount of Transfiguration with Jesus.

Do not be confused about Peter, James and John getting off on those special occasions. Jesus did not take them with Him because they were more spiritual than the others. They were an extremely human group. James and John were "sons of thunder." Men do not get names like "sons of thunder" because they are quiet! We have seen in scripture how ambitious they were. "Lord when you come to your kingdom"—of course they meant the literal kingdom that they anticipated at that particular moment—"let one of us sit on the left and one on your right hand." They wanted to be officials in Christ's government! They were aggressively political and ambitious. They were loud. Peter for his part was impetuous.

These are the three who went up the Mount of Transfiguration. They were chosen because Jewish law demanded that everything should be confirmed by the mouth of two or three witnesses. How else would we have had the story if the two or three witnesses had not gone there? We would have doubted the Mount of Transfiguration because we had no legal proof. But it happened and these three witnessed it.

What would you have done if you had been in Peter's position at this wonder of heaven's visitation? Jesus was radiant with the glory and splendor of heaven. He regained some of the glory that was his when he was with the Father before his Incarnation. Moses and Elijah, the great saints of the Old Testament, also appeared.

DOES GOD ACCEPT OUR HUMANITY

We cannot keep a man like Peter down! He is going to talk out even in the presence of Jesus, Moses, Elijah and when the gates of heaven are opened wide! "Lord let us build three tents, one for you, one for Moses and one for Elijah." He was very generous! He, James and John, he was certain, would be content to sleep on the outside without a tent, if they could just have the privilege of staying there.

Peter was a real human organizer, whether anyone asked him to or not. He was ready to organize the Old and New Testament characters even if in the process he was interrupting heaven's great revelation. This is such a human reaction. We do it in our churches. Sometimes we become so sure of ourselves that we take over and try to organize the Holy Spirit. If we would but wait a little longer until God acts who knows what things we might have to report! If Peter had not interrupted the dialogue that was taking place, who knows what further truths might have been recorded.

Jesus had to divert his attention to Peter and indicate the necessity to go down the mountain. At the foot of that mountain the other disciples were making a sorry mess trying to cast demons out of a little fellow who had been brought there by desperate parents. Jesus had gone and these disciples were trying and failing to do his work. Jesus seems to be saying to Peter and to the rest of us that getting to know Him does not mean that we must always be living at a high emotional, religious and spiritual peak. This is not normal. But we all seem to want this.

We have all had moments when we felt closer to God than any other time in our lives and our whole emotional being has been stirred and thrilled by the experience. If we could perpetuate this emotional experience all the time, we feel it would be great. It would not! There are demons in the world that need to be cast out, and that is never a pleasant task. There is work down the mountain that Jesus came to do and we must get on with it. He has handed it over to us who are believers to continue its performance. There are times when we must go up the mountain, but those times will be few and far between in contrast to the day-by-day, steady, dogged working, living and witnessing for Christ wherever we are.

We are so like Peter. Recall, too, the upper room. The disciples had been celebrating Passover and the Lord transformed part of it into the beautiful Communion service that we now observe. When it was over the Lord said, "You men are going to be offended because of me."

Even after this first communion service, Peter is still "running off at the mouth." "Lord, even if all the others around me forsake you, I will not forsake you. I'll die for you." Glib religious statements. We are all guilty of them. We even sing them, "I'll go where you want me to go dear Lord." As long as the Lord does not expect us to talk to our next door neighbor about Jesus, we will go wherever He asks us to go. We do not really mean much of what we say, and it would therefore be so much better if we did not say it at all. "Lord I will die for you." That is such an easy thing to say.

After Dunkirk, we were pastoring in England. Those were dreadful days, treacherous days and I recall one Monday morning when we had our pastors' conference. Our associational missionary had called us together and said, "Gentlemen, I have a question to ask you. The Germans may be here next Sunday. They have driven us from the mainland of Europe; they are bombing our cities at will. Wherever they have gone the first people to suffer and be put in jail are the pastors. Brethren, this morning we need to look into our hearts. If they do come to our little island this week, how many of you will report to your pulpits next Sunday?" The night before we had been up half the night with the screaming sirens and the roaring of bombers. In circumstances like these there are no easy words such as "Lord I'll die for you." I recall the spirit of prayer that day. Virtually every man had the same prayer, "Dear God, give me the courage to be in my pulpit next Sunday."

Peter said, "Lord I'll die for you." Jesus did not and does not expect us to talk like that. God does not ask us to make this kind of commitments. He knows of what we are made; he knows our weaknesses. Jesus told them what would happen. Not many hours afterwards, Peter is sitting there in the judgment hall. Give him credit that he followed at a safe distance! Most of us are still doing that to protect ourselves. A young woman comes and says that she knows Peter and that he is one of Jesus' men. He replies, "I don't even know Jesus." We can almost hear the echo coming from the Passover room. "I'll die for you." Another girl comes and says, "You are one of Jesus' disciples." Peter is getting a little wilder now. This happens when we are trying to protect ourselves. The third accuser comes along and by this time he is emoting and using profanity as he denies even knowing who Jesus is. She says that she can tell by his accent that he is from Galilee. Isn't it nice that even the disciples had accents.

We are all brave Christians until we are threatened. It is amazing what we do at these moments in order to save our skins. Peter lifted up his eyes and saw Jesus looking at him, and whatever was communicated in that look, Peter went outside and wept bitterly. You have done it too. The vacillation! Oh Lord, if we could only get some kind of stability into our Christian experience. We are not really going to get it. We are too human. Even when we are born again, we are not dehumanized. Some people think they are and try to act as if they are, but they become very unpleasant people to live with.

The resurrection morning came and some women were at the tomb and a young man gives them instructions. "He is not here, Jesus has risen." This blessed Son of God who has borne the sin of the whole world in his body on that middle cross and has shed his blood for the remission of our sin and who has grappled with hell to redeem us has come back from the dead. He remembers this miserable, vacillating, human called Peter by sending an angel to say, "Go tell my disciples and Peter that I will meet them in Galilee." Love of love, mercy of mercy, grace of grace! Peter, yes, the Peter who was cursing, swearing and denying his Lord to save his own skin! "Tell Peter that I want to see him."

Jesus encounters Peter by the lake side and says, "Peter, do you love me?" God is so gracious. If this were the average preacher he would start scolding Peter, telling him what a no-good kind of character he was to let Jesus down and do what he did to the blessed Son of God! We Christians today would be no better, we would take Peter and we would crucify him if it were happening in our society. Jesus said, "Peter, do you love me?" What a question.

There is a word play in the Greek that we do not see in the English translation. Jesus is using the wonderful word "agape." This kind of love is only possible in experience through the Holy Spirit. This is a word that means a commitment and resignation of the total person to another. Jesus in effect said, "Peter, do you love me so that your whole being is crying out for me?" Before Calvary and the mock trial you know what Peter would have said, don't you? "Oh, yes, Lord, I have agape." But Peter now replies using a different Greek word that we do not see in our version because both words are translated "love." Peter uses the Greek word "phileo."

The word "phileo" is a good neighbor word. It is affection. It is a "borrow-a-cup-of-sugar" relationship! So Peter when he hears, "Do you have agape for me?" replies, "Lord, I have phileo." Something has happened to our brother, Peter. He is no longer verbose about what he believes. And then Jesus asks a second time, "Do you have agape?" The second time Peter replies, "I have phileo." Jesus is making sure that this man is going to begin honestly in his relationship with Him.

The Bible says that Peter was grieved because the Lord asked the third time, "Do you love me?" If we read the Authorized Version we might think—and I have heard preachers saying it—that Peter was angry because the Lord kept pressing him. The Lord did not press him. Peter was grieved because the third time when Jesus asked the question, He no longer used "agape" but Peter's word "phileo." Peter had twice stated that he had "phileo" and Jesus was simply making certain that he really had that much for Him. Peter was grieved because Jesus, in spite of the miracle of Calvary, and the wonder of his person, had come down to Peter's level by using "phileo" instead of "agape." Jesus was trying to ascertain that Peter really could give him a pledge of even this affection. Peter having learned the futility of glibness could promise Jesus "phileo."

God, in Christ, took Peter with what he had! Later, at the day of Pentecost, God poured into Peter the oil of the Spirit which caught that spark of affection and set the wick of Peter's personality aflame so that he could preach the sermon which gathered in so many souls for the kingdom on that glorious first day of the Church.

Tradition tells us that at the end of Peter's life, the Romans, about to crucify him, offered him his freedom if he would deny Jesus. "I cannot deny Him nor am I fit to die like Him," said Peter, "Turn my cross upside down." Thus he died. "Phileo" had become "agape" through the Holy Spirit.

Here is the proof that God does not expect or demand the impossible from those who would serve him. Here is certification that our continuing weaknesses do not end the divine care for our souls. Here it is, clearly shown, the patient loving tenderness and understanding by God of the Human dilemma. What more need be said to reassure us in our humanity that God is committed to us.

CHAPTER 4

Putting Life in Healthy Perspective

"Not as though I had already attained, either were already perfect; but I follow after, if that I may apprehend that for which also I am apprehended of Christ Jesus. Brethren, I count not myself to have apprehended; but this one thing I do, forgetting those things which are behind, and reaching unto those things which are before, I press toward the mark of the prize of the high calling of God in Christ Jesus" (Philippians 3:12).

For Paul this was not only a time of looking back but also anticipating the future. He was approaching the end of his life. I suppose there may be some virtue in indulging in the practice. However, I would like for us to consider these words in a context relative to our spiritual health.

One of the perplexities confronting Christians is the discrepancy between what we would like to be and what in fact we are. We yearn to be better men and women but somehow or other we simply do not meet the ideals we have set before ourselves. The wonderful thing about Revelation is that it understands our humanity. We cannot emphasize this enough. The Bible is not nearly as hard on us as we are on ourselves!

I'M HUMAN—THANK GOD

There are so many external forces that play upon our humanity shaping our lives. In his book, *Human Nature Under God*, Dr. Oren Baker notes some of these when he says:

"In large or complex societies the chief form of control is institutional although custom, dictating distinctions of right and wrong, continues to play an important part.

"Institutions are arrangements for patterning behavior of individuals—in world history five have persisted and continue to do duty:

      a) The Family
      b) The State
      c) Industry
      d) The School
      e) The church (or its counterpart)

" . . . Each of these is a complex of human behavior of wide variation and is also the patterning of that behavior with them" (p. 190).

We can readily see that for believers there are built-in conflicts in this list. There is little or not interrelation between these institutions to coordinate them into a single purpose. Thus there are inherent conflicts introduced into the life of the human exposed to them.

The Church has indeed influenced all of these institutions either directly or indirectly over the centuries. Its influence has been felt at every level and some of our culture does reflect that influence. At our present stage of social development contemporary humans may not recognize the Church's past involvement. We take so many socially effective mores for granted yet they are the results of centuries of Church influence. Secular society has taken over many of the functions previously the exclusive territory of the Church. The result is that many look on them as secular and have no knowledge of their origin.

The unrelatedness of the modern evangelical church to life has unfortunately widened the gap between Church and society so that it may never be bridged. To protect itself under fire, the evangelical church has withdrawn itself from the modern social dialogue. This is of course a sign of insecurity concerning its faith. It is also a sad reflection on evangelical leaders who use excuses like sanctification as a means of withdrawal. Their real motivation is protection!

The cumulative effects of family, state, industry and education are simply too much for the Church to combat by withdrawal. This is why we have lost the world's ear. The answer to this problem is total and quick involvement of the Church at all social levels.

All of these institutions have their own kinds of legalism to mold society. People are addicted to methods. Books on "How to . . . " are popular. This easily moves into the field of Christianity. Some of the criteria are irrelevant but persistent in their demands. The believer is caught in the uncoordinated "pulls" of all of these institutions and their legalisms both cultural and religious. The ensuing frustrations can be overwhelming to the point of surrender to circumstances.

It is true that we have built into us a propensity for legalism. It is much easier to resort to Judaism than to live by faith! I suspect that this is true of all men—

I'M HUMAN—THANK GOD

Christians or not. They say, "tell me how to live," "tell me what I ought to do." To tell men precisely what they ought to do is legalism, it is Judaism; but we all yearn for it. We want it because we need an objective pattern. It may be also that it is a constant reminder, as Paul indicates, that we are failures. Legalism always tells us that we have failed. Any kind of legalism will ultimately frustrate us. Thus, frustration is built up in our lives.

Paul was not a man of pious platitudes, in spite of his greatness. He was a man who was constantly aware of his deficiencies. In descriptive language, for example, he talks about "fighting a good fight." This is the language of a boxer. Boxing is not exactly tranquility! He also uses the language of the knight in his armor complete with breastplate, sword and helmet, as he goes out to the conflict. This is not exactly the language of tranquility either!

In this context which we are considering, Paul puts himself in the spiritual olympic games and particularly, the marathon race, the cross-country race. This is not a relaxing experience! No matter which figure Paul uses, he is struggling with the fact that there is a difference between what he wants to be and his humanness. He never excuses his sin, but he is aware that it is there. Paul was no perfectionist.

As a pastor I find more and more people who confess the name of Christ discouraged and frustrated with their lives. Many of them have even given up any idea of Christian service and involvement, not because they do not want to be involved but because there is a constant sense of guilt because of their inadequacies. They are so frustrated with the human experience of having become Christians, but not having become perfect. How can we bridge these conflicts and still find peace for our souls?

Paul intelligently recognizes that he has not apprehended, nor is he perfect. The word perfect should be translated "complete." We are not complete in our lives. Paul observed the past and the present, then said, "brethren, I count not myself to have apprehended." The word he uses for "count" indicates a reasonable process. He is in prison and it is as if he has made two columns and in one he has listed his spiritual assets while in the other, his debits. He has added these up, and now declares, "Brethren, I simply have not made it in my experience." What is he going to do about it?

"I count not myself to have apprehended." Paul is being honest. We all tend to be hypocrites. If we were not, the frustration of imperfection would destroy us. We pretend to be what we are not. Thus, in our legalistic spiritual tendencies, we look at other people and find they are not quite as good as we are. This brings comfort to us and we immediately set ourselves up as experts of spirituality!

I'm not much of a golfer but on one or two occasions I have managed to par a hole. Only one or two occasions, I assure you! I recall that when I did par a hole, and when my partner was making a mess of it, I immediately became an expert in telling him how to do it! Have you ever noticed this tendency when you succeed at something, even coincidentally? We immediately become experts on how to do it! People are spiritually like this. Whatever spiritual success they have, they become tutors of the rest of us. The reason is that they find comfort for their own frustrations in another's deficiency. They become critical. We do not find Paul like this. Paul does not criticize people because they are not as he is. What better person than Paul could, from a human point of view, say, "Brethren, I have made it"?

Paul wrote most of the New Testament. He tells us that he was received up into the third heaven and saw things no other man has ever seen. God revealed them to him so that he might impart them to us in revelation. Here is a man who was spiritually and intellectually above his peers. Here is a man who soared to giddy heights like a spiritual eagle, reaching realms that we know nothing of, yet he could say at the end of his life, "Brethren, I count not myself to have apprehended."

You see we must learn that what we are before God is never because of what we ourselves are, but always because of who Jesus is. Our relationship with God is not determined by what we have done nor what we are now doing. We are not saved by works, nor does our salvation continue upon our works. "The life that I now live, " says Paul, "I live by faith of the Son of God who loved me and gave himself for me."

The just man—the man who is counted righteous before God—is counted righteous by his faith in Jesus Christ, and not by the conduct of his life! It is hard to believe this but this is only because we all tend to be legalistic. We all want to contribute our own activities. But judicially there is nothing we can do. Jesus has done it all. This relationship with God, once it is secure in our hearts through our faith in Jesus Christ, is a continuing, perpetual experience of grace, forever and ever.

Paul is being very logical about it when he says,

PUTTING LIFE IN HEALTHY PERSPECTIVE

"brethren I count not." He could have permanently put his head in his hands and cried, "what a wretched man I am." "I'm not the kind of man who ought to go to church today." "I've done the wrong things this week." "I'm not going to teach a Sunday School class." "I'm not the kind of person I ought to be." "I've failed!" "I think about my past and I don't feel the least bit worthy to walk with God, much less serve God." That would be an evil attitude and represents the greatest area of defeat in the life of the average believer.

Paul's second important step is to determine what to do about the situation. "This one thing I do, forgetting those things which are behind." Now there is a difficult proposition!

God says, "I have blotted out thy sins as a thick cloud." He says, "I remember your sins no more." Then, why is it that, having confessed and been cleansed through our faith in Jesus Christ, we believers do not also forget? Believers, having confessed their sins before God's presence are immediately and perpetually kept clean by the provisions of Calvary. God forgets what we confess! If God forgets, that is all we need to be concerned with. Why should we remember it anymore? If we do remember it and allow it to condemn and build up guilt and fears that will frustrate us in our living and scorn us in our witnessing, we are insulting Calvary, as well as robbing ourselves of mental health. So Paul says, "Forgetting those things that are behind."

It is not, however, the forgetfulness that simply ignores. It is the forgetfulness of discarding, putting it off. I remember some old suits that I have but I am not wearing anymore. This is the kind of forgetfulness we mean. These suits are not a part of my person anymore. Luther put it well in his *Thirty Nine Thesis*, when he said, "the whole of the Christian life is a continual attitude of repentance." We should be living in the perpetual provision of the miracle of grace through the atonement of our Lord Jesus Christ and the power of his resurrection.

There are many problems involved in Christian happiness right at this point. Many Christians have not found the art of forgetting what they have confessed. They do not forgive themselves. There is no need for this; nor is there any virtue in remembering our sin. Peter had a blunt Eastern way of putting it when he suggested that the forgiven and cleansed man who returns to his forgiven sin is like "The dog turned to his own vomit again, and the sow that was washed to her wallowing in the mire."

Why wallow in sin even by the thought of it! Live in the freedom of sin forgiven. This is the thrill of Christianity. We need to tell it to the world. We need to repeat it to ourselves every day. Too often the pulpit ministry has been legalistic and constantly emphasizing our faults and errors. It is very easy to tabulate categories of sin so that all of us can become overwhelmed with guilt and shame. This insults the Gospel!

The message of the Gospel is not that we wallow in the mud or the mire of sin, but that we seek the cleansing that is perpetually available in Christ. We must not become preoccupied with our errors but rather confess them and move on.

I had a Presbyterian professor in Scotland who used to say to us, "Gentlemen, do not talk too much about the Devil because if you do he will get you." I rather suspect that this is what Paul is trying to get over to us. "As a man thinketh in his heart, so is he." Whoever thinks a lot about sin is going to get it!

Paul says, "Forgetting those things which are behind I reach forth for those things which are before." He is continuing the figure of the marathon Olympic race. Paul sees himself running a race the extent of which is from the beginning of his Christian experience to the end. Nowhere between the beginning and the ending are we through. We are only through when we have reached the finishing tape. Anywhere between, we have nothing to brag about. The man ten yards ahead of us is no more there than the man ten yards behind him. So we cannot look back and criticize others. The process of running the race is our Christian experience.

I love Sunday School picnics. I love to see the little ones racing and getting awards. They are great little creatures. I have never failed to see the little Primaries in a race, whose mommies and daddies were not more concerned than they about their winning! Mommy and Daddy usually advise the children, "whenever the man says go, you run. Run for your dear life and get up there and win." It seldom fails that one of the children starts off successfully and then wonders if maybe he is doing the wrong thing, and stops to look back. Everybody in the race shoots past him and the race is lost! This is the kind of thing Paul had in mind.

We are not at the finishing tape so let us keep on running. "I count not myself to have apprehended" means simply we have not yet concluded the race. Therefore, we must not be preoccupied with the past. We must forget that river we forded back there; those thorns which hurt us; that mountain we climbed. The moment we stop running to think about these things, we fail to progress. The moment we sit down, we lose the race. So we cannot be preoccupied with our successes or failures. We must keep on going on. We are not through until we get there. So we stubbed our spiritual toe back there! Do we want to spend the rest of our lives regretting it? Then we shall never reach the finishing tape. Get up, go on with God depending on the provision that he has made for us in Jesus.

I will never forget the first experience I had in high school learning to walk the bar. The first trip we made, we all fell. I remember our gym teacher went to the other end of the beam, took a piece of chalk and made a cross on the post supporting the bar. "I want you to get up there, and I want you to imagine you have a whole sidewalk under you and start walking," he instructed. Now that sounded good! I was particularly anxious for I was the first one to go on top and try out the method. Amazingly enough, it worked. I got up and looked at the chalk mark on the other post and walked right across and never had another problem. You see, the first time we were all preoccupied with the difficulty of the path we were treading. Once we get preoccupied with our problems and look down at our feet our problems will crush us.

Paul concludes his philosophy on this subject by saying, "reaching forth unto the things which are before I press towards the mark for the prize." The prize is the upward calling of God in Christ Jesus. I believe this refers to the second advent of Christ. We do not have the right to stop. Everything between our decision for Christ and the end of our Christian journey is by faith in the provision of Calvary!

Paul states his purpose, "that I might be found in Christ, not having my own righteousness (which is legalistic) but that righteousness (imputed) which is by faith in our Lord Jesus Christ."

It matters not how perplexed you feel, how guilt ridden, "if we confess our sins, He is faithful and just to forgive us and cleanse us from all unrighteousness." Do it, and when you do it, walk out with the stateliness of a child of God, clean, whole and uncondemned, either by God or yourself. This is the peace of God.

CHAPTER 5

Depressive Holiness

Martin Luther wrote, "when I was a monk I thought I was utterly cast away, if at anytime I felt the lust of the flesh; that is to say, if I felt any evil motion, fleshly lust, wrath, hatred or envy against any brother. I assayed many ways to help to quiet my conscience but it would not be for the concupiscence and lust of my flesh did always return so that I could not rest but was continually vexed—but if I had rightly understood these sentences of Paul, "the flesh lusteth contrary to the Spirit; the Spirit contrary to the flesh; and these two are one against another so that ye cannot do the things that ye would do," I should not have so miserably tormented myself but should have thought and said to myself, as now I commonly do, "Martin, thou shalt not utterly be without sin for thou hast flesh; thou shalt therefore feel the battle thereof" (*Commentary on Galations*).

Luther later in the same article quoted Staupitz who said, "I have vowed unto God above a thousand times that I would become a better man; but I never performed that which I vowed—Unless, therefore, God be favorable and 'merciful' unto me for Christ's sake, I shall not be able with all my vows and all my good deeds to stand before him."

Bunyan struggled hard to find peace in his soul in

the ambivalence between the awareness of evil as a human fact and religious idealism as a yearning of the heart. He wrote of his problem thus:

> My peace would be in and out twenty times a day; comfort now and trouble presently; peace now and before I could go a furlong as full of guilt and fear as ever heart could hold. (Quoted by Wm. James, *Varieties of Religious Experience*, p. 186).

This kind of depressive holiness is not proof of piety but the true gospel. The gospel is precisely to relieve this human dilemma not to accentuate it. We can understand this depressive religious experience prior to an awakening to salvation but when it persists it is depression of a sort that perverts Christianity. There is no virtue in such misery.

This kind of depressive holiness is not proof of piety but certification of misunderstanding of the gospel even as Luther suggested in the above quotation. This attitude can make no contribution whatsoever to our relationship with God. It can, however, and does do emotional damage to our person. A morbid spiritual approach to our humanity is useless as a contribution to a happy life. It arises from a misconception of the gospel message and can be either a neurotic or psychotic condition in the person.

The misunderstanding of the atonement is another factor involved in this kind of spiritual morbidity. Weakness of faith in Christ's atonement created by a sense of guilt and a lack in personal contribution to salvation often causes people to spiritually afflict themselves in order to create a sense of contribution either to their repentance or atonement. This produces a depressive holiness which has no real effect upon salvation except to pervert its purpose and place the person in bondage. However, it does produce for some a sense of contribution to their salvation by self-induced emotional punishment.

Almost everyone of us finds it difficult to accept the formula, "The just shall live by faith." There is something in our make-up that resists the free offer of grace. Perhaps it is because we are commercially disoriented to the idea of something for nothing. For this reason most of us desire to contribute what we conceive to be religious acts in order to justify our acceptance by God. Of course if we would only think about it we would realize from experience the futility of the endeavor especially when it is measured against the holiness of God.

At the other end of the spectrum of this type of religious experience is the overly scrupulous Pharisaical and judgmental type who is a misery to himself and a sorrow to all who know him. He too is embarked upon a program of self-redemption which he seeks to prove to others by playing judge over them. This person creates a miserable ambivalence in his person. Outwardly he gives the impression of holiness while inwardly he is out of fellowship with God. This too is a total misconception of holiness. For one thing this person has suppressed any sense of personal guilt by a mental blindspot to the reality of his own spiritual condition. He is really fooling himself about his holiness. It is a self-constructed condition producing a mental incapacity to see himself as others see him.

What I call pornographic preaching is another depressive method used to foster guilt which will hopefully create for the evangelist who uses it the emotional atmosphere which he considers spiritual revival. He goes down the categories of sin often unwittingly placing the emphasis where his own personal problems are. If with these he is unusually descriptive it may be that he is being autobiographical. So much of the "holiness" type of preaching falls into this category. It places salvation exclusively on the basis of sins of commitment thus emphasizing the symptoms rather than the disease.

The weakness of the foregoing type of ministry is that sooner or later, followed to its logical conclusion, it takes in everyone including the preacher since perfection is not possible even for him. It is like the "dog returning to its vomit and the pig wallowing in the mud."

God receives no honor by the propagation of evil pursuits descriptively portrayed in varying degrees of sordidness and sometimes by an almost inordinate pride of "having been there."

None of us needs to be reminded of the depths of evil for it is evident. Some argue that it is only a presentation of the facts in society but it seems to me that there are many "facts" in society that we do not need to underscore.

It is like a playwright I learned of who was justifying to a friend his "X-rated" play by arguing that he was only portraying life as it really is. His friend quickly reminded him that throwing-up when one is sick is part of life but who wants to pay to come and see it happen!

The redemptive act of God in Christ does not need this approach especially after salvation has been obtained. Redemption is healing for the soul. Healing is not helped by aggravating the wounds. There are moments of conviction of the Holy Spirit that are real enough but coming from Him they will always be in the context of love and assurance of cleansing.

Confession of sin is only for believers. It is undertaken before God and not men. Confession to each other is as foolish as victims of the same disease comparing symptoms. It makes for interesting conversation but does nothing for the cure of the disease. Obviously one diseased person cannot cure the other.

There is a psychological context where talking out one's problem with a professional can be helpful but this is usually only required when the problem has become neurotic or psychotic. This is not confession in the biblical sense.

The Greek word for confession is "homologos." It means, literally, to have the same reason or mind with the person to whom the confession is made. Let me illustrate.

Some years ago I saw my first basketball game in St. Louis. Now and again the referee would blow the whistle and one of the players would raise his hand. I soon discovered that this player was agreeing with the referee's judgment that he was the guilty one in a foul play. This is exactly the meaning of confession as related to the believer's sin. The Holy Spirit calls the "foul" and our personal identification with it before God produces his promised cleansing.

I'M HUMAN—THANK GOD

Paul teaches us in I Cor. 11:31 that self-analysis and confession before God or our apparent weaknesses will exempt us from any chastisement necessary by God. Fear is thus removed and honesty invoked on the part of every one of us. Paul does not recommend morbid introspection but honest assessment and confession to keep our fellowship with God open.

Self-analysis before God is not self-punishment. It is precisely to exempt us from punishment that Paul recommends it. "For if we would judge ourselves we should not be judged (by the Lord)."

Self-punishment for sin is a futile and unscriptural thing. No amount of it makes any difference before God. Jesus bore our sins in his own body at Calvary.

Calvary is made of no avail by those, however well meaning, who imagine they can create their own spiritual health.

Paul had to deal with this problem in his own life for it is a constant human error that must be overcome if we are to live in the blessing of spiritual freedom.

Holiness is spiritual health. The spiritually healthy person will have an intimate spiritual relationship with God. It includes moral and mental health. It is also a wholesome well-adjusted personality possessing an enviable attraction to those who do not yet possess it. This is a witness to the world of meaningful values and not merely verbal persuasion. This concept of holiness knows how to accept life as a reality but lives in the freedom of God's provision for human failure. It is freedom from condemnation and freedom to live meaningfully.

CHAPTER 6

A Christian by
Standards or Faith

Very often the error of "standards" is that they are built on a wrong concept of God. This wrong concept creates a God whose views are little better than elevated human opinion, either our own or some religious leader whom we follow. He too may be completely wrong. He may well project his own personal dilemma into his teachings.

I recall a true story quoted by a good friend who is an outstanding theologian. He visited the campus of a fundamentalist Bible school some years ago out of due consideration for the president whom he had known in his younger days. Walking the campus my friend noticed that the young women students wore dresses almost alike and down to their ankles. He had previously heard of his friend's extremes. He asked why this unnatural procedure only to be honestly informed by the president that when he was a young man the legs of young women were a source of temptation to him! So a whole group of young people were affected by this man's personal weaknesses. One could be expelled from this school as unspiritual for breaking the rules. This is not as extreme as it appears for there are many areas like this.

I'M HUMAN—THANK GOD

Notions of God's person range from gross sacrilege to threatening superstition. Sometimes we take anthropomorphic (giving God human parts like hands, feet, etc., when in reality He is a Spirit having no bodily parts) language that is meant only to communicate *ideas* about his person and literalize them. God then becomes a super-human; a super-man, bigger and better than the best man we know. Because of this literalizing, God is accredited with human characteristics blown up to our own ideas of perfection. In all of these we have really constructed an idol. There are many sincere and deeply religious people whose concept of God is thus self-constructed. It was Brunner who said, "The God whom I can think for myself is for that reason an idol" (*God-Man*, p. 57).

This process of thinking has done almost irreparable damage to the work of the ministry and of the Church. Too often if anyone deviates from our construction of God he becomes apostate to us and we close our ears to what he has to say. This way we build a protective wall around our human-divine relationship and thus never grow. This way we can comfortably handle God. He, of course, has lost his true identity. For one thing he is no longer infinite except we interpret that word quantitatively and then he is as we have said only bigger than the biggest human we can think of.

God makes judgements, of this we are universally sure. But what kind of judgements does he make? Here too is the danger of the self-constructed God. So often He is made to adopt our value judgments. We consider that if we are against something he surely will cooperate and curse what we curse and bless what we bless whether or not we have his permission.

But are our value judgments valid? Where did we get them? Are they not in fact largely products of our culture? Do we have the right to judge those in another culture by ours? Who is to decide who is right? So the questions pour in great profusion. These unanswered questions, even when suppressed, become part of our uncertainty and create spiritual frustrations.

"Theology is not a free-for-all; it is man's science, his understanding of God and all things in their relation to God. It is not, however, every man's science. While method prevents totalitarian ambitions on the part of any individual theologian it should also underscore the empty ambitions of those who reduce theology to theologizing on their own religious experience as if thematizing ones own religious experience was all there is to doing theology." (Wm. E. Reiser—Paper "Lonergan's View of Theology," *Scottish Journal of Theology*, Feb., 1972).

We must realize the colossal limitations placed upon us by the very nature of the idea of God. "God is a Spirit" declared Jesus. The Westminister Confession adds ". . . having no bodily parts." This is why it is easier for us to comprehend God in Christ. The Incarnation gives us about as much as we can humanly, meaningfully and realistically conceive of God.

When we have said this we have to admit that Jesus while having the "fullness of the Godhead" nevertheless humbled himself from that stature and in that condition of Incarnation restricted his true glory. Thus, at the end of his life, he anticipates his resurrection to the environment of the Father by praying, "Glorify thou now me with the glory which I had with thee before the world was" (John 17).

God, in his true person, cannot be contained within either theology or personal thought processes. At best, even with Jesus, we only have a glimpse of his greatness and glory.

Revelation gives us about all we can contain but it leaves us standing, as it were, at the edge of space with its immeasurable distances even in light years. We would do well, then, not to bring this Being into human confinement in social, moral or cultural problems.

The Holiness of God, under the foregoing terms, is equally a measureless thing. It is inconceivable for it demands his infinity. The only thing we can be sure of within its meaning is separation from all humanly conceived notions of the word.

The holiness of God is that which we as humans offend. We have obviously no other inherent choice in the matter. The alienation is total and involves all nature of which man is a part in spite of his reluctance to accept it.

The holiness of God is the only absolute in terms of righteousness. It is equally obvious that, by these terms, man has no human possibility of the absolute. He may constantly remind himself that he is "short of the glory of God," but he will never be anything else in experience, saved or not.

Emil Brunner commenting on this said, "So non-Christian religions know something of the sin of man but only as an accidental not as an essential . . . Where sin is known as an essential characteristic, religion comes to an end and the only thing left is that God himself should remove sin. And these two characteristics, the cessation of religion and the removal of sin by God alone, are peculiar to Christian faith" (*God-Man*, p. 150).

This is the position of real life separated from the idealistic dreaming of theologians particularly of the Armenian persuasion.

To quote Brunner again, "The man in the street . . . all these know much more of the real life of the soul of man than any scientific psychologist whether he be idealist or naturalist or romantic philosopher of identity" (*Ibid.* p. 147).

If the foregoing is true, then obviously we must depend upon God's exclusive grace and mercy both before and after we are regenerated.

Regeneration gives us new capacities by the transcendent gift of God the Holy Spirit, but does not ever make us gods! Imputation is the only answer to a continuing relationship with God.

He who desires a continuing relationship with God will strive to please, not to obtain salvation by virtue nor to have it continue by virtue of works of any kind. Before the holiness of God there is simply nothing we can do to impress Him with our holiness.

Our living in the family of God after the new birth will establish conduct as family identity with the Father but not as a means of keeping alive in the family. Such a thought is preposterous and heretical.

To what purpose then do we strive in Christian living? First of all we do have new life in the Spirit. This removes the innertness of being "dead in trespasses and in sin." Thus being made alive with God we now have capacities of response to the divine purpose. These are capacities that do not remove our humanness but rather modify the natural acts and introduce distinctly spiritual acts.

There will always be, of necessity, tensions within the believer between his natural self and the Spirit within him. We can only, healthily, cope with these tensions if we recognize that our relationship with God is secure through faith and imputation. This having been done we can proceed to the business of life and growth in grace. Where grace is recognized as the free gift of God to unworthy people the phrase "growth in grace" means I am developing within the gift. Developing within the gift of God perpetually keeps the believer in need of Him and his provision. Thus, "the life that I now live (as opposed to before salvation) I live by the faith of the Son of God who loved me and gave himself for me."

There are cultural factors by which we must live because we are social beings. These we collectively endorse for our own harmony of living. Some of these however are unreal for they vary from place to place. Christian groups also develop cultural patterns that are the reflection of bygone leadership rather than the work of the Holy Spirit.

Any believer who has traveled and worked in church groups around the world knows the futility of these "standards." In parts of the world believers engage in conduct condemned by believers in other parts of the world. The norm has been established as we indicated earlier by Christian leaders who perpetrate their own weaknesses.

Some years ago we attended a summer conference where mixed swimming was for some peculiar reason frowned upon. My wife and I innocently put on our swim suits and set out for the lake only to be stopped and reprimanded for our conduct. We accosted the leader of the conference who informed us that he, personally, did not go along with this foolishness. We reminded him (it was a married couples conference by the way) that we had slept together for over twenty years and what in the world would swimming together do to our Christian life! Later a vote was taken and unanimously the nonsense was dispensed with. Everyone knew it was foolishness but went along hypocritically although they did not believe in it!

We simply must remember that in the final analysis it is our individual relationship to the Father that is important. Our collective, social, responses in the modern world are already well-defined by the influence of Christianity over our society over the centuries. It was one thing for New Testament Christians in a totally pagan world to stand out, "separate," because of Christianity. Now-a-days the modern world accepts as a matter of fact certain social standards of conduct unconscious that they are the products of centuries of Christian influence.

It is for this reason that good unregenerate citizens look as good as regenerate ones in public life. In fact all too often the only assurance of difference is the believer's faith in his experience and the acceptance of that faith by God. In other words, the difference between the believer and the unbeliever is known more from God's perspective than ours. There are of course cultures not permeated by Christianity where this is not so. However, modern culture has influenced even these.

I'M HUMAN—THANK GOD

Too often we contrive our experience to point out that we are different. This really can become ridiculously ambivalent and even humorous to the intelligent observer. All of the legalistic endeavors to make Christians dress differently, or wear their coiffeurs differently or ignore the normal pleasures of life because the "world" also enjoys them are aids to spiritual slavery serving no good purpose but to frustrate the lives of still more people.

We write these lines because of thirty years of pastoral experience dealing with frustrated believers who do not enjoy their Christianity and are morbid in ambivalence between life as they want to live it and as it is being thrust upon them by well-meaning but mistaken leaders. Neurosis and psychosis have developed for many of these. They will not give up Christianity but they live in superstitious fears as great as the heathen.

Anders Nygren said, " . . . the righteousness of God which comes upon Christians is not an inner quality of man's but an objective power (from God)" (quoted by David Cox, "Jung and St. Paul" p. 16).

Moral perfection is not a human possibility if the measurement is against the holiness of God. This is the only justifiable scale permitted in the Scripture. All else is relative.

Suppose we set up a hypothetical scale on a line from zero to one hundred in which the one hundred represents the holiness of God. Each of us could then mark off where we think we are but no one would dare in his sanity place himself with God. Therefore no matter at which point we place ourselves we still are dependent upon the grace of God.

The process is reluctantly suggested as an illustration for as we have noted the holiness of God is infinite in quality beyond human comprehension which makes it even more ridiculous for us to measure our relationship to God by any other means than grace and imputation. The gift of salvation then truly takes on the wonder and miracle that rightfully belongs to it.

Continuing the scale analogy for a moment, we must now ask are we more or less children of God by our position on the scale or are we all the same before God?

We suggest that if as Paul indicated in Romans 3:23, "There is no difference for that all have sinned" so likewise in redemption there is no difference in relationship for that all who believe are saved.

Sanctification is the name for spiritual growth and development of the believer. It is a process of accomplishment and maturity. But sanctification is not my relationship to God as his born one so much as it is my fellowship with God as his child. The difference is essential. Some still need the sincere milk of the Word while others have advanced to spiritual meat. All are equally his children by grace.

In any natural family whenever the teenager exalts himself above the baby in the family status, he is foolish and immature. Rather he assists the less-developed remembering the care that was given to him in the same situation. So too is the family of God. Realizing that no matter where we place ourselves on the imaginary scale, we simply are not anything. We hesitate to be critical or judgemental of those whom we consider less on the scale even though we have no scriptural justification for such a value judgment of another member of the family of God. Such procedures are in themselves arrogant before the facts of experience and ought to silence us.

Christianity is a blessed reality that has often been made an unnecessary burden by misconceptions on the part of those who would be Pharisaical towards their brethren. Peter tried to settle this once and for all at the Council in Jerusalem, (Acts 15:8ff):

"And God, which knoweth the hearts, bore them witness, giving them the Holy Ghost, even as he did unto us;

"And put no difference between us and them, purifying their hearts by faith.

"Now, therefore, why tempt ye God to put a yoke upon the neck of the disciples which neither our fathers nor we were able to bear?

"But we believe that through Christ we shall be saved, even as they."

It is too bad that in each generation there have been those who insist on reverting to Judaism.

CHAPTER 7

As The Shepherd Sees the Sheep

I suppose Psalm 23 is a favorite portion of Scripture for most of us who know the Bible at all, and even those who are not acquainted with all of the message of the Scripture find great comfort in the poetry of this Psalm. It is a poem that has reached the highest expression of faith, both in the Old and the New Testaments. It is also a useful means to point up the divine responsibility for our human needs.

The Psalm is part of a trinity. The 22nd, 23rd and the 24th Psalms together form a trinity that tells us of the Messiah. That is to say that centuries before the coming of the Messiah, these forecast concerning Him. You will recognize for example the familiar verse one of the 22nd Psalm, "My God, my God, why hast thou forsaken me," as being the words from the Cross.

The 22nd Psalm gives us a picture of Jesus, the Saviour. The 23rd Psalm, which we are to consider, presents a concurrent picture of Christ in the world as the shepherd or the pastor. The third Psalm of the group, the 24th, reveals the consummation of the age in which the Messiah becomes King.

We are primarily concerned in this context with the

present ministry of Christ in the Holy Spirit through the
agencies of the Church and through the ministry of the
under-shepherds.

If the 23rd Psalm tells us of the contemporary ministry of the Messiah, the pastor, then it is also true that
he fulfills much of this ministry through the under-shepherds or pastors whom he has ordained to feed the flock.
But our present interest in the 23rd Psalm is not so much
to emphasize the human pastoral ministry but because it
speaks simply of the interest of God in Christ, in each
of our lives.

We are observing the practical concern of God for
our humanity. We are also seeking to strengthen our
faith and confidence in our relationship to him. The
23rd Psalm delivers a message of positive health for every believer.

The Psalm is built very much like a problem of Eu-
clid, a theorem of geometry. It has an hypothesis: "Jehovah is my pastor." We then follow along in the Psalm to
prove this hypothesis. Finally, in the 6th verse, "Surely
goodness and mercy will follow me all the days of my
life," we have the great *Quod Erat Demonstrandum.*

Jehovah is my Pastor. Jehovah. What do we mean
by this? Who is this great Yahweh spoken of in the Old
Testament? What is the meaning of the word? If we
can, indeed, understand the implications of the hypothesis that Jehovah is Pastor, then we can be assured of the
effectiveness of the rest of the Psalm.

Yahweh! You remember when Moses stood beside
the burning bush and God was commissioning him to
deliver the people of Israel from Egypt? You recall Moses was stunned and stuttered before God that he did

not want this particular ministry. One of his last arguments against fulfilling the ministry was, "When I go to these people, whom shall I say sent me?" He recognized that he simply could not approach these people in captivity and say, "I'm here to deliver you." Someone would be sure to ask, "Who are you and who sent you?" For this reason God gave Moses His great name of authority, "Say that I AM THAT I AM hath sent you." Now we cannot, for certain, give all the implications of the name Yahweh hidden in this statement. We know something about it, however.

We know, first of all, that it means that Yahweh, in his person, is the God of all past. Not simply the past of history, but going back and beyond the beginning of time and creation. Going where our minds cannot reach with certainty. Going to an area of thinking, a dimension of thinking, that is almost totally incomprehensible to humans. Going back of the universe, Yahweh is from eternity. Eternity is not time multiplied to infinity. No, God dwells in another dimension from time altogether. Time is a little part of eternity marked out for the convenience of human beings. That information is as much as we can function with. Jehovah is not merely the God of the past, in terms of time and history, he is back and beyond all the mystery and wonder of our creation This is one facet of the meaning of Yahweh.

Secondly, Jehovah is the God of the "here and now." He is a contemporary God. He is presently involved in the universe and beyond. He is involved in time and space. He is involved in history. He is not transcendental to the extreme that he is away out there with no interest in you and me. He is a God who is involved in the world. He became, for example, flesh and dwelt among us. He moved into historical experience, into human experience, becoming flesh he entered through infancy. He passed through the stages of primaries, juniors, adolescents and adults. He moved through the stages of human development. God moves and lives among us and with us. God understands time and history. He understands the pressures that are upon humans. "He is tempted," says the scripture, "in all of his faculties like we humans are, yet without sin." So, Yahweh is the contemporary being. He is eternal, but he is also involved in time. He is involved with you and me.

The third implication of the word Yahweh is, that he is the God of the future. Here again, it is not simply the future of history to the consummation of the world as we conceive it, but beyond that to eternity ahead. God is real, active, intelligent and in absolute control. This is the Lord who is the pastor. What a pastor! There certainly can be no competition here at all.

This concept of Jehovah is humbling to those of us who dare—dare—to say we are called to be under-shepherds, under-pastors. This concept will rob a pastor of any inordinate egocentricity if he will only think for a moment of what is involved in the person of God in Christ and in the Holy Spirit. The Trinity is involved. That we have the privilege of serving under him is a miracle of grace!

Now we have the hypothesis, Jesus is my pastor. Because of the implications we have just observed in his person, "I shall not want." You have heard this said before. The New Testament repeats the idea when it says, "My God shall supply all your need, according to his riches in glory, by Christ Jesus." We talk glibly about God being our shepherd and that we shall not want. We say it but few of us believe it. We have a sneaking suspicion that when we say it we had better get in on the act ourselves because, if we don't, he may let us down. And so we bolster our faith by our own energies.

"I shall not want." There is another thing we Christians do with the idea of the God who can supply our needs. We put our needs at the lowest possible level, supposedly for God's convenience, so that he may the more easily overcome the difficulties! Really, it is to satisfy our own lack of faith. We say God supplies our needs and we would feel quite satisfied if the promise was met by the very minimum standards we can think of. We would consider this, Were our needs being met? But if this God is all we have just described then it is downright insulting to him when we set our vision any lower than the best we can be with him and for him.

It is not merely things. We do think of these too easily. The ministry of God in Christ which is contemporary meets the total need of humanity. He ministers to us in our mental and emotional problems. He ministers to us in our physical needs, material needs, personal needs, psychological needs, business needs, family needs, home needs or study needs. God in Christ is in all that is you, whatever and wherever you are involved. He is your pastor at every possible level. He is there for anything that is human; for any event. He is your pastor at every possible level. I shall not want because I have this kind of pastor.

"He makes me to lie down in green pastures and leads me beside the quiet waters."

I'M HUMAN—THANK GOD

David was a shepherd boy before he was a king, and the experience of this Psalm was his as a shepherd with his sheep. It is beautiful how God, in inspiration, took men with what they had and translated it into revelation. David knew how sheep enjoyed the experience of being made to lie down. We must keep clear the figure of the sheep and the shepherd in this Psalm. He makes me to lie down in green pastures.

One of the problems God has with Christians is to get them to "be still and know that I am God." This is one of the perplexing problems of Twenty-first Century Christianity. We must learn to "come ye yourselves apart and rest awhile." We are living in an activist society. Our churches are activistic. We do not think we are doing anything for God unless we are doing. If we could only learn that sometimes we are doing the most for God when we are doing nothing but simply waiting in his presence. This is so difficult for those of us who are oriented to go, go, go, work, work, work. To be still and to be able to stand ourselves long enough until God can communicate with us is a great and necessary discipline!

For the sheep, the source of relaxation—the green grass—is also the source of food. This is equally true for us, if we will follow the Shepherd. The compelled relaxation instead of merely being physical is also mental and spiritual food. And as we relax we grow in grace and in the knowledge of the Lord. God is trying to compel us to take time out from our schedule so that he can talk to us. I think that we will admit that God himself has quite a schedule! But being our pastor, he insists that we learn to lie down in the green pastures and beside the quiet waters.

AS THE SHEPHERD SEES THE SHEEP

I know when we are in a hustle and bustle we insist we can pray to God, but the most we can say is "Hi Lord!" Unfortunately, some of us are content with this! God, in these terms, is about as important to us as a neighbor whom we meet walking down the street! The divine Shepherd will not settle for this kind of relationship. He wants us to learn the art of getting alone and listening. It is good for mental health. It is good for physical health, and it is excellent for spiritual health. This is holiness.

"He restoreth my soul."

The business of living is spiritually exhausting. Christian business men and women know this. Business can sap spiritual energy from a person's soul faster than anything. And mother, you must admit that a family can sap the spirituality out of you in a real hurry. You can rise in the morning with the fruits of the Spirit high in your thinking processes and by the time the children have gone to school and your husband has gone to work, you wonder if you ever knew what the fruits of the Spirit were! The ordinary course of events weakens spiritual energy. Students know that those professors can sometimes be extremely demanding upon their spiritual resources, but not nearly as much as students are demanding on the professors' resources!

We are simply saying that normal day-to-day experience, can be so spiritually exhausting that we sometimes feel like giving up. If we can learn to come apart and rest awhile, the spiritual restoration we gain will reinvigorate us to live for God, so that we can go out and face the new day. One mother I know says that the best time for her to fellowship with God is in the morning after everybody has gone and she has time to sit down and have a cup of coffee. The coffee gives her a little physical stimulant, and then as she meditates the Lord takes care of the rest! But we need to do it! It is essential that we do it for our own spiritual well being.

"He leads me in the paths of righteousness . . . "

Now we have action again. "He leads me in paths of righteousness for his name's sake." Notice it is, "for his name's sake." It is for the convenience of the shepherd that he chooses the right path, not necessarily the convenience of the sheep. Jesus says the same kind of thing when he says, "Let your light so shine before men that they may see your good works and glorify your Father which is in heaven." This is very disappointing to the person who is centered in himself. This kind of person thinks righteousness is to make them good citizens or so that folks might notice how wonderful they are! As believers, our motivation for living is in order that men when they do see our good works will not credit them to us but rather our Father. The implication is that they recognize the change in us as divinely given. And so the shepherd leads us in paths of righteousness for his name's sake.

"Yea, though I walk through the valley of the shadow of death, I will fear no evil."

In those days the sheep were led down the mountain paths and, as the shepherd walked ahead of his sheep, wild lions and other wild animals would come out of the thickets and pounce on the sheep. So, this is not a funeral verse! This is a verse of life and experience. It is not death, but the constant threat of it that is spoken of here.

AS THE SHEPHERD SEES THE SHEEP

As the sheep followed the shepherd down the mountainside, now and again an animal would come out and threaten the flock. The sheep say, "I will fear no evil. Thy rod and they staff they comfort me." The shepherd used the crook. That crook is the rod and staff. Now he uses it as a weapon—now he uses it to latch around the neck of the sheep and pull it out of danger. But the sheep's attitude is, "I can relax with those wild animals around me because it is the responsibility of the shepherd to take care of me." In the New Testament Paul says, "We are killed all the day long." He is simply saying that the world in which we live is a constant threat to our spiritual life. Everything about it is a threat to spirituality, and so we are walking in the shadow of constant threat, but we have the promise of the Shepherd that he is by our side as defender. It is in the midst of our enemies that believers are spiritually sustained by the shepherd of our souls.

"He anoints my head with oil."

When we think about the sheep, we wonder what oil has to do with them. In Scotland where I grew up we had lots of sheep. I don't know how many of you have ever heard of sheep-dip. I have tried all kinds of ways to get the meaning of this little portion of scripture consistent with the figure of speech used. Most commentators depart from the figure of speech. I know the shepherds in Scotland use sheep-dip, a messy substance. When sheep are out in the pasture, they get bugs, ticks and lice and these are downright uncomfortable to live with.

Shepherds periodically bring the sheep into the pen and anoint them with the sheep-dip. It destroys the bugs so that the irritation ends and the sheep can begin to relax again. The Psalmist notes that this is what the

I'M HUMAN—THANK GOD

Pastor does for us in our day-to-day experience!

I like the way the young people say it today, "What's bugging you?" Let us face it, it is the multiplication of all the little irritants that are the real threat to our spiritual health and holiness. It is the little things, multiplied together, that keep getting to us. If we will only allow him the shepherd will anoint us and destroy these irritants that "bug" us and give us the ability to walk with him.

How about that as effective proof of our hypothesis? Now we can set down the declaration that our hypothesis is demonstrated in a practical fashion.

"Surely goodness and mercy shall follow me all the days of my life"—and when it is ended—"I shall dwell in the house of the Lord forever."

So we learn another dimension of living the Christian life that accounts and provides for our humanity.

CHAPTER 8

Man Must Think Positively

In Philippians, chapter four, verse six, Paul says, "Be careful for nothing." (This is the old usage of the word "careful" not the modern usage.) Paul is really exhorting us not to be full of worry, concern or anxiety over things that are happening around us, but:

> In everything by prayer and thanksgiving with supplication to let our requests be made known unto God, and the peace of God which passes all understanding shall keep our hearts and minds through Christ Jesus. And finally brethren, whatsoever things are true, whatsoever things are honest, whatsoever things are just, whatsoever things are pure, whatsoever things are lovely, whatsoever things are of good report, if there be any virtuous things, if there are any worthy things, think on these things.

We tried earlier to show the apostle Paul's concern with the experience of his humanness although a believer. He was able to correlate his life experiences in relationship to God. There is still sin in us after we are born of the Spirit of God. We still have error in our ways and make mistakes. What are we going to do with these discrepancies? They must not threaten our relatedness to Christ for our security is not built on our works. Our security is built on the eternal sacrifice of Jesus on

I'M HUMAN—THANK GOD

Calvary. All that Jesus accomplished at Calvary is perpetually and eternally propitiating for the sin of the whole world and for the believer. The eternal reservoir (if we may use that phrase) of atonement is inexhaustible and it is this that gives us eternal security and not our conduct. Our faith is in that eternal provision. If it depends on us then, of course, we shall remain frustrated, miserable and wretched in our experience. So we must learn to live by our faith. We learn to live by faith that imputes to us, or charges to our account, the righteousness of God through Jesus Christ. The apostle John notes that we are "accepted in the well-beloved." We are accepted in the person of Jesus Christ. We have placed ourselves in Jesus, in his person. We have transferred our interests to Jesus.

Some years ago we were leaving Pennsylvania for a new pastorate. We owned our home there and as time came to move we had not yet sold it. We went to see our attorney about our problem and he informed us that it was no problem at all. He asked us to sign the appropriate papers giving him power of attorney. I had heard of power of attorney. But supposing he did a bad deal, would I have to live with it? He replied more positively that if we were to transact a good deal, we would live with that! He pointed out that he received personally no benefit from a good deal. "Then you are really telling me, sir," I said, "that when I give you power of attorney I take all of my person and all of my thought processes in relationship to this home and this sale, and invest them all in your action so that whatever you do carries the same authority as if I had done it myself?" He said, "Absolutely." This is the principle of salvation through faith in Jesus Christ!

MAN MUST THINK POSITIVELY

All that is essential for our well-being forever in relationship to God, the eternal judge, we have invested in the custody of Jesus. He is our power of attorney forever and ever. We have, as it were, signed the documents by faith and He is our power of attorney. We need no longer be concerned about our eternal salvation. God wants it that way in order that we do not spend our time being fearful and anxious, wondering if we are saved or not. We simply rest in a completed, finished, ultimate task that assures us that Jesus is at the right hand of God the Father.

This salvation is as sure as the Resurrection and can never be reversed at any point, at any time. The strength of this faith is that it removes anxieties and fears we may have about eternity. We must now be concerned about the present. We must now get on with the job of living, day by day.

What then is the significance of Christian living day by day? We do not live the Christian way in order to go to heaven. We do not go to heaven by anything that we do. We will go to heaven because "Jesus is the way, the truth, and the life and no man cometh to the Father except by Him." What are we to live a Christian life for? There appears to be only one reason why biblically, every believer who accepts Jesus Christ as Saviour, is not immediately transferred to heaven and that is that we may remain on earth as God's witnesses. Of course there is the discipline of learning to grow in grace and knowledge of the Lord, but that is something apart and separate from eternal security.

Anything that we do as believers after we have entered into a relationship with Christ, is in order to glorify our Father. Since he is our Father, we are his children. We are his family living in this world witnessing to the glory of the family, the benefits of the family, the thrill of the family, the happiness of the family, the joy of the family, the fellowship and sharing of the family. This is what makes Christianity such an exciting, enthusiastic wonderful thing. If we belong to Jesus, then we belong to each other. I need you, you need me, we need each other. Here is why we have a community of believers called the local church. We do not exist simply to have an organization setting up business procedures like a department store and for the sake of competition with the Methodists across the street. We are here as groups of believers, of like mind, because we are part of a family. We belong to each other. We are born of the same spirit. Our daily living only becomes a problem when we fail to recognize who we are, as redeemed persons, and our interrelatedness to every other believer.

We become spiritual dual-personalities after salvation. We are compelled to continue living with all that goes into the makeup of our background, including genetic structure. We must live with the things we blame our grandparents for. Our daughters once caught the habit of blaming what they are on their parents. We tried to remind them that we too came with a medical package and so we could blame our grandparents too!

There is little we can do with what we are genetically. Temperamentally some people are nice, quiet and loving. That does not mean that they are more spiritual. It simply signifies that is the way they were born. If you are such a person, do not feel virtuous about it. Some of the rest of us were born like James and John, the sons of thunder! There is nothing virtuous about that either. What sons of thunder some of us are! We bring all of this bundle of character traits to our Christian experience. We do not lose our individual identity. In other words, when we become Christians, we are not ever dehumanized. It is when we try to act dehumanized and prove we are artificially spiritual, that we become absurd and repulsive. The worst witnesses in the world are the people who are self-conscious of their goodness. They develop an arrogance and put-on which everyone knows does not fit. It is a bothersome thing. It is just not real! It is not human. These become so heavenly-minded that they are no earthly good. But the Bible makes if firm and clear that we retain our humanness together with the Spirit of God.

Most of us would like a categorical list of things we can do in order to be good Christians. If we were to produce such a list we would destroy the very principle that "the just shall live by faith." Let me illustrate what I mean.

John came home one night. Mary opened the door and the way it opened conveyed an immediate message to John that something was wrong with Mary. She walked into the kitchen and John said to himself, "Ah, I've got to find out about this." He went into the kitchen and said, "Darling, is there something wrong?" "Oh no, no nothing wrong," she said. You know how women do this, don't you? This is a woman-made trick! So John tried being nice for a while and finally gave up in frustration. Tears began to come down Mary's cheeks. Finally John had enough and said, "Now look, I'm not ignoring this, what is wrong?" "Oh, I had coffee with

Susan this morning." Mary began, "do you know what Bill did last night? He came home and, for no reason at all, brought her a bouquet of flowers. It was not their anniversary, it was not her birthday, he just loved her, and brought flowers home. You've never done that for me. You don't love me." Well, it took the rest of the night to straighten out that kind of illogical thinking.

Next night, John came to the door bearing a bouquet of flowers! Mary took one look at him, banged the door and began to cry. In amazement John said, "Well, now, what have I done?" She said, "You only brought me those flowers because I told you Bill brought flowers the night before. You don't really love me, you're just trying to copy Bill."

Bill brought flowers out of the spontaneity of love. John brought flowers because it seemed the thing to copy. They both brought flowers but only one bunch of flowers was a product of inner experience. That is the difference between faith and legalism. Do you catch it?

We can copy Christian things, and on the outside it may look like we are doing what is the real Christian thing but it is not, for our motivations are wrong. When God judges us, he looks into the heart of us.

The Sermon on the Mount is built on the premise that the motivation of the believer is much more important than the activity of the believer. This is why Jesus uses language such as "out of his innermost being shall flow rivers of living water." God does not want people copying Jesus. The "Imitation of Christ" may be good reading, but it is bad theology. We do not want to parrot Jesus. We do want the life of Jesus to live in us.

MAN MUST THINK POSITIVELY

Because it is life and he is the source of life, it is spontaneous. It is the outgoing of the Holy Spirit in our lives. It is not any form of legalism. It is spontaneity. It is Christ living in us and not our living according to a pattern somebody has told us to observe.

Some years ago in England we succeeded a pastor who was one of those aggressive fundamentalists. There is nothing wrong with the fundamentals. It is some fundamentalists who are the problem! This particular man was so aggressive that he split the church. He moved up the street and rented a school house and started a competing church. It is always difficult to understand the morality behind this kind of situation.

Next to our parsonage there lived a very dear, precious, old lady who was a member of one of the great British missionary families. She had a very lovely lady companion. We became very fast friends with these two. The old lady loved our little daughter and loved to have her come into the house. She loved to see the little children playing and laughing. It was exciting. There was one problem. She had moved her membership to the splinter church believing that the man was right. It did not alter our relationship with the dear old lady. She would constantly mention the schismatic pastor's name, and say that he was such a dear man because he came by to see her every day. He lived two or three doors down.

One day I was at a pastors' conference, and this pastor was there. We were having lunch, and he was quite loud. It did not take my ears long to pick up that he was talking about our dear old lady whom he visited every day. He was telling some of the pastors that she had him in her will for a new automobile when she died, and that was worth a visit every day. I was born a son of thunder! God has, through the years, given me a lot of grace and a lot of sense, but that day I nearly lost my good sense because there is nothing that bothers me more than that kind of pastor. I could have disillusioned the dear old lady, but I did not. She was very old. I thought that when he was through with his automobile, he would have to look in to the eyes of Jesus, the Chief Shepherd, and I wondered if the ill-gotten automobile would be worth it.

The pastor's motives were wrong. It was a good thing to visit with the old lady every day. It was a Christian pastoral thing to do, but in his heart his motive was wicked. You see what we mean? Pure motivation is what we are trying to emphasize in our Christian living.

The scriptures make it very clear that having become believers, the important thing is now programmed thinking. Programmed thinking! "As a man thinketh in his heart, so is he." Thought processes, what is going on inside, are the center of the real person. We too easily think that man is flesh and blood. This is why some mourn so desperately at funerals. They have misunderstood or simply do not believe the Bible. We are not merely flesh and blood. These bodies are only the containers in which we are living. The real person lives inside this container. We are spiritual persons. This is why we must go inside to get to ourselves. This is why, when the Lord judges us, he does not observe the container. Some containers are very attractive but inside are poisonous. So the Lord searches the heart. He sees the spiritual self. He knows that this is the center of what we are. Jesus can say, "It is out of the heart that evil proceeds." The heart is used in Bible psychology as the spiritual center. It is out of this that all sins are committed. It is equally true, that out of this part of me as it is yielded to God there comes all the virtues of the fruits of the Spirit; love, peace, joy, longsuffering, gentleness, meekness and so on. Thus we must not give objective rules because these would not be realistic.

If God, the Holy Spirit, is in us, and he is if we are believers, then let him work in us and we will do what he is doing in us. The normal work of the Holy Spirit is love, joy, peace, longsuffering, gentleness, meekness. As the young people say, "This is how the Holy Spirit does his thing." When we are yielded to him, out of the inside of us, where he is, will come his works. In the measure that this does not occur is the measure that we are falling back on our natural self. This is where the believers' battle begins. How do I combat it? I have to fight this battle, and we will study more of these things as we go on.

In Philippians, chapter 2 and verse 5, the apostle Paul says, "Let this mind be also in you." See how he keeps going inside? He does not ask us to copy Jesus but rather, "Let this mind be also in you which was in Christ Jesus." The Greek word used for "mind" in this context (There are different Greek words used for "mind" in the New Testament, they are not all the same although they are translated the same in English.) is a word that speaks of the control-tower in the mind. It is the will, the determination, the attitude. We could translate, "Let this attitude be also in you which was in Jesus Christ" or "Let your regenerated inner-spirit become the motivating factor." Let the Holy spirit control this power center in your life.

I'M HUMAN—THANK GOD

Paul shows us how to program ourselves for Christian happiness: "Whatsoever things are true, whatsoever things are honest, etc., think on these things."

The power of positive thinking is a genuine scriptural message after we are born of the Spirit. It is not a genuine possibility until we are born of the Spirit. It seems to me that positive thinking is impossible when we are, by nature, sinners and separated from God. The only real positive thing in the world is all that is pure in God through Christ. When we possess God in Christ and the Holy Spirit is within us, we then have the capacity to think positively, spiritually. As Paul says, we can think with the mind of Christ. We can begin to program ourselves, program our thoughts, our inner-selves for what our lives should be.

I was talking about this sometime ago to some young people and one of them came to me afterwards and said, "That takes all the joy out of life." I asked why and he said, "Well there are a lot of things you can't do." "Who said so?" You see we have the wrong attitude about God. We assume that God is disinterested in the world, in business, in government or in education. We exclude God from what we call the secular. For the believer, there should be no such thing as the secular. Everything is spiritually significant. If it is not, then we are not believers in the biblical perspective. Do you think Jesus would have been interested in watching a ball game? I find it difficult to get positive response when I suggest this! We have a false idea that God has no interest in this kind of thing. I think we are hopelessly wrong. The other Sunday we had a football game on television and I really did wonder what Jesus would have done about the game if He were here. I have an idea Jesus would have said, "Enjoy the game and I'll meet you over on the edge of town for a group meeting about an hour after it ends." I cannot think he was as tied and restricted to time schedules as we are.

When we talk about programmed spirituality and programmed thinking, do not get it into your mind that, in order to be spiritual, we must always be talking about God and the Bible. It is not true. That would be abnormal. We love our wives, gentlemen, but we do not spend all day talking about them. If we did, that would be a sure-fire sign that there was something wrong with the relationship. We can go about our tasks, and while they involve our relationships with God, wives and our families, they are all related to our spiritual lives. Meeting needs of family, home, health, education and recreation are all spiritual pursuits.

When Jesus told the parable about the talents which would help men work and multiply, he took the process out of mere secularity. The one who was condemned, buried his talent fearing his master did not want him to get involved in this kind of thing. So when we talk about spiritual involvement, do not think that we are asking you to live in a convent, or be unnatural, or oddballs in society. We must not be! The truly normal person is the one who belongs to Jesus Christ. Paul advises us to program our thinking process. Whatsoever things are true especially in connection with doctrine, think about this kind of thing.

Whatsoever things are honest, whatever things can be revered and respected, think on these things.

Whatever is just. The Bible uses the word "just" to mean imputed righteousness. We are to charge righteousness to other people. All of these things are related to people. Charge righteous things to their account, not bad things.

"Whatsoever things are pure, and whatsoever things are lovely." There is a beautiful word used here for lovely that means face to face with affection for people. Christians should positively cultivate people. We Christians should be personally and culturally elegant and distinctive. This should be not only in terms of what we call spiritual things, but also in our dress, our homes, our demeanor and our cultural interests. We should be God's ladies and gentlemen. This I believe is Christianity working itself out from the inside of us.

"Whatever is of good report," is the kind of thing to think about. Never mind the gossiping prattle of the people who by gossiping display their lack of spirituality. The next time someone wants to gossip and give you a bad report on another tell them their carnality is showing. They won't call you again! They will have to find someone who is as carnal as they are to listen.

We must program ourselves this way. The direction will come form within and we must obey it. Gossiping is doing damage to other people, but not as much as it does to our own spirit. It weakens us spiritually. So Paul advises us to listen for the good report and the virtuous things. Some people are constantly looking for evil and demons. How about looking around you? If we can observe things that are worthy of praise then we should fill our minds with these things.

These processes will help us become effective Christians, and produce happiness in our living experience. Neglect of this teaching is why so many Christians are miserable. They have not realized that the Christian life is a total life which demands total programming. To everything that we are, as parents, as children, in school, in business, in the home, in the community, in the nation, in government, in economics, we must bring the positive life of the spirit. Even a cup of water can be transformed to a miracle of grace provided it is given willingly in the person of Jesus Christ.

CHAPTER 9

Re-Programming the Believer

A new life demands programming to foster its interaction with its environment, other people and with itself.

The new life must have a good image of itself if it hopes to be helpful and meaningful to other lives. It takes the spirit of a man to understand a man just as it takes the Spirit of God to understand God. The new life in Christ combines these two factors.

Understanding our own humanity assists us in our understanding of other humans. With the Spirit of God we can learn to know God's attitudes to men and become the transmitters of God among men. Knowing God by his grace means to be indwelt by his Spirit. We therefore have the capacity to translate the things of God which we can receive as spiritually reborn ones to other humans who cannot comprehend them because they do not have the Spirit of God. This is the significance and the imperative of witnessing.

To be effective communicators of God will require the renewal of the person who has been regenerated to bring him into conformity with the life of the Spirit. This is the process of sanctification. The natural human processes of growth and development are brought over into the spiritual by Paul in a very practical program.

I'M HUMAN—THANK GOD

There is no need for "other-worldish" mystery and sanctimonious emoting to bring it about. What God desires of us as believers is not in heaven to be brought down, but in us to be brought out.

Let us look at Paul's letter to the Romans, chapter 12, and verses 1 and 2.

> I beseech you therefore, brethren, by the mercies of God, that ye present your bodies a living sacrifice, holy, acceptable unto God, which is your reasonable service. And be not conformed to this world; but be ye transformed by the renewing of your mind, that ye may prove what is that good, and acceptable, and perfect, will of God.

We want these chapters to be very practical concerning Christian living. I don't know of any two verses that give us a better program of Christian growth and development, than these in Romans 12:1-2. In order to make them effective in their progression, I want to treat them in reverse order of subject matter because it is in this order, from the end of the second verse backwards, that we do in fact get the precise meaning and order of Christian growth and development.

The first motivating factor in Christian growth should be "that you may know the good, acceptable and complete will of God." This is the sum total of Christian living. This is basic to any meaningful relationship we may have with God. To know the complete purpose of God is the ultimate of happiness.

When we talk about the will of God it introduces strange ideas to our thinking. The will of God used to be for me, as a young person, a very confusing matter. It usually meant "Lord, where do you want me to go?" "Lord, what do you want me to do?" "Lord, what do you want me to say?" In fact, the will of God was totally egocentric thing! It was me, me, me! It was so concentrated on the self it took years to see that anything that concentrated on the self was, in fact, unspiritual. To think that the whole will of God, the complete will of God, as Paul expresses it, is centered around our personality is of course an absurdity.

Paul's presuppositions are:

(1) There is God.
(2) That God has created the world and those who dwell in it.
(3) God has total purpose for all that he has created in nature, human and non-human.

Paul will later say (in the 13th chapter) that God has a purpose for governments, even if it's not the party we voted for! God has a significant purpose in all of history. The world is not going on by chance. There is a consummating factor in the purpose of God, and everything that is happening, although not necessarily approved, He will make it work out for the ultimate good, which is his purpose. The ultimate purpose is the consummation of the world in the establishment of the Kingdom of God on earth.

God also has a purpose in nature. When we talk about ecology, as long as we are not involved in the absurdities and extravagancies of the subject, we should believe that it is part of the divine plan that we have sense in using and not abusing God's creation. This is also part of the divine purpose.

I'M HUMAN—THANK GOD

God has a destiny for his Church, collectively. He has a purpose for the Church.

In the measure that God is involved in his universe, in government, in nature, in the church, He is also involved in the life of the individual but only when the life of the individual fits into the total pattern of all that God is endeavoring to accomplish. We cannot function independently, on our own. We have a responsibility to our spouses, to our families at large, to the people of God in the assembly of believers. Wherever God places us we have a responsibility. We have a responsibility to the community. The more we move in this sphere of thinking, the more we begin to realize that we cannot function on our own, separated from all the other factors of the divine interest. Therefore, the total and complete purpose of God will relate to his total purpose for the Church, family, community, nations, and the ultimate consummation that He has in mind. We ourselves have, of course, a distinctive purpose within the context of this total will of God for the world.

This view is much more exciting than prating our feeble egocentric requests. If we pray to be in the great divine overview of all history, and the eternal purpose that He has decreed from before the foundation of the world; if there is a place where we can fit in; if there is a niche for us to coordinate ourselves, our talents, our gifts and our persons with his total purpose, then we can expect the Lord to count us in.

This gives the will of God a totally different perspective. It also makes us very deeply conscious that we are significant persons not merely in relationship to ourselves, but to the total community of people in the world. God still loves the world, you know!

In order to come to this experience, Paul lays out certain very practical things that must take place. Paul is assuming that a person has come to know Christ before these things can become effective. A person who does not know Christ is not born of the Spirit of God and has no intelligent understanding with God's purpose.

In Ephesians, chapter two and verse one, Paul says that before we came to know Christ, we were "dead in trespasses and in sin." Dead people don't do anything, don't feel anything and can't be anything! This is spiritually true. A person who has not been quickened, made alive, by the dynamic of the Spirit of God, has no real relationship with God except possibly an intellectual acceptance that there may be a God. Even the devil has this! This is something we need to see as distinctive in Christian teaching. It is not enough for a man to say that he believes in God. The devils and demons believe, and tremble, declares the Scripture. It is by the miracle of grace that a real transaction takes place in our lives and God, the Holy Spirit, touches us in our inner man. Thus we become awakened and alive toward God and spiritual values.

Frankly, this is also why becoming a Christian makes life just a little more complicated than when we were not Christians. It is always much easier, in some ways, to be dead than alive! This is why Job prayed that he might be dead. This is why in frustration, at some time or another, many wish they could be dead.

To be spiritually quickened and alive in God and aware of the world purpose in Him is to be aware that there is a great transaction taking place in history around us. That we are now part of it and can share in it is one of the most exciting things of the Christian gospel. When we realize that this truth also contains in it the sublime element that we shall never die, then there is no end to what we begin on earth. Jesus says, "I am the resurrection and the life. He that believes in me, though he were dead, yet he shall live and whosoever lives and believeth in me shall never die."

We begin to see ourselves then as strong spiritual beings living within bodily containers. That which lives within the container cannot be destroyed by the forces of Hell. It is this that is the significant thought behind Jesus' statement that the Gates of Hell cannot prevail against the professing Christian. When Peter said, "Thou art the Messiah, the son of the living God." Jesus said that on this confession He would build his church. Does one's spirit not confirm that it is on the confession of the Lordship of Jesus that we become Christians? "If thou shalt confess with thy mouth the Lord Jesus and believe in thine heart that God has raised him from dead, thou shalt be saved." Spiritually the Gates of Hell cannot prevail against us and we shall never really die. If we believe this, it will give force, strength, and purpose to living.

We must not view ourselves within the context of a few paltry insignificant years on earth. We do not see ourselves as Shakespeare suggests, coming in from one wing of life's stage, playing our little part, and then going out the other. This is not so, for what we as Christians play on the stage continues where the world cannot see it. The Mount of Transfiguration proves this for us. After the passing of the centuries, Moses and Elijah are still involved with Jesus in world events. It is excit-ing! To deal in the total perspective of this new life, is a heavy responsibility on us. Before we became Chris-tians there was little we could do about it.

Some think they have the self-determination to be saved. They do not. The Bible says that the foundation of salvation is the confession that Jesus Christ is the Lord. We never could make it on our own for the Bible tells us that "no man can confess that Jesus is Lord, save by the Holy Spirit." We may talk about it intellectually, but we have not experienced it until the Holy Spirit has touched us. This is a divine truth. It is also why we must be careful about morally persuading people into accept-ing a creed that means they are saved. We have done this with too many. These have been morally persuad-ed, intellectually persuaded, to accept a creed and have never had the quickening spirit of God touch their souls. This is why we have, in most of our churches, only 50% of the people genuinely involved. Far too many others became involved in a kind of mass promotional scheme to talk them into church membership.

When someone is quickened by the Holy Spirit, he knows it, and he will never enjoy being separated from the fellowship of the believers. There are not too many who really know the Lord who enjoy never being in church or having anything to do with it!

The tragedy of those sold on moral persuasion is a deep concern. It is a major problem yet to be faced by statistically hungry preachers who have gotten peo-ple into this unhappy condition for the sake of count-ing them. It will be the sorriest sight of all at the day of judgment when statistically oriented evangelists or preachers have to look on thousands of people whom they emotionally talked into decisions to satisfy their ego and so-called success, are turned from heaven's door. This will surely be the most shameful judgment of all. This is the most frightening thing in my heart as a preacher of the gospel. A plague on statistics! Let us make sure that any who make decisions really know what it is to be born again!

Where do we go from the new birth? We are to start renewing our minds but how in the world do we begin to do this?

When I was a young Christian, I thought the idea was to go into my bedroom and pray, and the more I prayed and dreamed and concentrated (almost in the formula of a seance) I mentally hoped that something would break through in the room and I might hear voices, or something really mystical would take place. There are so many Christians like this. They feel something miraculous has to take place before God comes close. Exactly the opposite is the truth! Jesus said that people who are constantly looking for signs are the weakest. It takes a mature believer to believe, live and walk in what he believes without the constant emotional excitement of the supernatural.

Paul gives a practical solution when he says, "renew your mind." We are now alive unto God, we are not dead in trespasses and sin; therefore, we have personal responsibility to renew our minds. How do we do it?

The Greek has no word for brains. Isn't that a co-incidence? We must not, therefore, assume that God is against the idea, since, after all, they were his idea to begin with! Some of us would like to be excused on the matter! In contrast to English, the Greek uses several different words for the varying facets of what we call the brain. There is a word "nous" used in Romans 12:2 to denote the learning processes. It is an important little word and it is the one we shall be most concerned with.

There is another word used in the New Testament and, unfortunately, also translated with the word "mind." It is unfortunate because "mind" does not convey the meaning. For example, in Hebrews, chapter eight, verse ten, there is a quotation from the Old Testament, "For this is the covenant that I will make with the house of Israel after those days, saith the Lord, I will put my laws in their mind." But he uses another Greek word for mind "dianoia." This word means "appetite." It is the word that would be used of hunger, or even sexual appetite. It does not contain the concept of learning that is in the earlier word. This is a word describing human cravings. God says that He will put a craving in our hearts for Him, an appetite for Him. This is part of the word of grace.

The word, "dianoia," is also used in a negative, sinful sense. In Ephesians, chapter two and verse three, the word is used in the evil sense, "among whom we also had our conversation in times past in the lust of our flesh fulfilling the desires of our nature and of our minds." The appetites spring up from within and the flesh fulfills them. So the word, "mind" can be used in this negative sense also.

There is yet another word in Romans, chapter eight and verse five, "For they that are after the flesh (that is unregenerate human nature) do mind the things of human nature, but they who are after the spirit, the things of the spirit, for to be carnally minded is death, but to be spiritually minded is life and peace." Here the word used is "phroneo." This is the idea of the head being the control tower of what we do.

I once tried riding a horse and that was the last time! I was having problems with the horse. I felt at such a disadvantage perched up between heaven and earth and at the mercy of this creature! But whatever it was, I was doing something wrong with the head, and I remember the fellow who was standing by shouting at me vigorously, "Give him his head." We have taken that phrase figuratively and brought it into human experience and this word would denote this kind of action.

The word that we are most concerned with, however, is the word "nous" referring to the learning process. How do we renew our minds so that we can become computerized to be the kind of person who is geared into the complete purpose of God? Anyone who is born again is a new babe in Christ. The Bible gives us complete authority to make an analogy between natural birth and growth and spiritual rebirth and growth.

Let us have a lesson in elementary learning processes then we shall discover how to renew our minds. I shall illustrate it by telling about our first-born. Of course, all of this is not in time sequence, but collided together for effect. Now remember that!

When my wife had gone off to the hospital to have our first child, I prepared a nursery in our home, next to the master bedroom. We had water put in and spent time and money getting nursery furniture. We painted the place and it was stunning. When my wife came home, I showed her this beautiful room and she was thrilled! That night, at bedtime, there was the baby being brought into the master bedroom. I inquired of my wife,

"Where are you taking the baby?" "Well, you can't let that little one sleep by herself over there in the nursery." I replied, "She did it at the hospital, didn't she?" "Well, this is different. We are not going to have that," she responded. We had quite a lengthy discussion, and finally the baby went in the nursery! We knew the baby was comfortable. We had learned that much, to see that no pins were open and all that kind of thing. She was fed and quiet and comfortable and the temperature was right. We had organized everything to bring this baby up by the book! My wife had other ideas. Remember I am colliding a lot of this sequence!

Somewhere in the middle of the night, in fact not too far into the night, the baby began to feel something. It doesn't know too much yet. It was learning. It was what the psychologists call visceral, something in the stomach. The little creature does not know enough to know what to do about the matter except cry, and so it begins to scream and cry. Like a shot and before I could say anything, my wife was out of bed, over the wooden floor, and when she got to the nursery switched the light on. She went over to the baby, touched the baby, and in a moment or two, put a bottle in the mouth. The baby became quiet! Mother felt very virtuous at what she had done. When I had a chance to communicate with her, I said, "That is your first mistake!"

The baby had already renewed its mind concerning physical feelings. A few nights later, the baby gets the same feeling, so it knows what to do! It yells out! Mother is up and makes the noise of footsteps on the floor and baby stops crying. Mother tiptoes back to bed. Isn't that beautiful? She is hardly in bed till baby starts again and mother is out again. This time she gets the light on, and baby stops crying. She tiptoes back again. What she does not know is that baby has renewed its mind! It had learned through its senses. It had heard footsteps on the floor. That was the first stimulus. Then the light on the eyes! That was the second stimulus! Then the touch, then the tasting, etc. Through her physical senses her mind had been renewed by these stimuli. Of course, what happened after awhile was that she heard the first stimulus and had enough sense to quit crying, because she expected the other stimuli to follow. Mother had not learned this for she came back to bed after the first stimulus thinking the baby was being real decent about it by ceasing to cry.

This is exactly what the New Testament means by renewing your mind, as a believer. After we come to know Christ we must begin feeding into our minds things that are spiritual and approved by God. This is what Jesus meant when he said, "If your eye offend you, pluck it out." He did not mean us to go literally popping eyeballs all over the place! He was simply saying that if through our eyes there is conveyed to our minds that which is programming our conduct to evil then quit looking! Get rid of it. "If your hand offend you, cut it off," said Jesus. He is again referring to the program of mental renewal. If, through the sense of touch, there is conveyed to our mental processes that which will cause us to live contrary to the total purpose of God, then quit touching. Thus the program of mental renewal, under the direction of the Spirit, becomes an imperative in practical growth and development.

We are not recommending censorship in the sense

RE-PROGRAMMING THE BELIEVER

that I was raised where we even had a library committee in our church who had to read the books before we could read them. Everybody wanted on the library committee! They were the only ones who had freedom to read everything and yet have the spiritual sanction of the church for doing it!

The only justifiable censor is the conviction of the Holy Spirit. He is within us and we will find that when we are engaging in some questionable area He will point the finger at us from within. When He does, quit! Whatever it may be, this should always be the guiding principle. It should never be the legalism of well-intentioned preachers. They say one man's meat is another man's poison. This is true. There may be things that are tolerable in one life and would not create spiritual problems but those same things may be very wrong for another life. This is why we cannot generalize laws. This is why we must listen to the Holy Spirit for He will always speak in relationship to who we are and how we are constituted. This is important so do not copy another Christian. Listen to what God is saying within. Use his word and feed on it. He will guide us. There are many things in the scriptures that will give direction as to where we should go. This is why, if we do not read the Bible we shall never know. The Word of God is a living thing which in conjunction with the Holy Spirit makes effective in our lives the divine pattern.

The fellowship of believers is also essential to the renewing of our mind. People of like mind strengthen each other. It is so much easier when we are sitting in the stands at a football game to shout for our team when all the people around us are supporting our team.

I'M HUMAN—THANK GOD

Two or three years ago when we were at a Hurricane game in Miami, we found ourselves seated, for some reason, right in the midst of the Notre Dame supporters. Do you know how difficult it was to shout for the Miami Hurricanes? We never had so many "dirty" looks in all our lives! On the other side of the field where the Hurricane supporters were, everybody was in fellowship! The fellowship of kindred spirits is an important thing to strengthen our determination. This is as practical as we know how to put it.

CHAPTER 10

Transformation

We have seen how a new baby learns to renew its mind by the learning process. Through its senses, its receptors, it receives into itself many impressions which govern its conduct. There will of course be added features. There will be imitations later on as it looks at its parents, brothers, sisters and even later as it observes its peers. All of these will be received into and renew the mind. These will build character and conduct.

When we are born of the Spirit of God we become new creations. Something as real has happened to us as in physical birth. I find it amazing that there are those who are still of the opinion that to be spiritually re-born is mere acceptance of a creed or that it means to believe or practice certain things. This excludes the possibility of a divine act; that something has subjectively taken place. Many in our churches are not enjoying the Christian life because it is merely a creed to them. It is not an experience. They are subscribing to something objective to themselves.

I was once expelled from the Kiwanis Club because I missed four weeks. You know, it is harder to be a Kiwanian than a church member! If you do not pay your dues, they dismiss you and if you do not attend regularly they dismiss you. They do not make any apologies about it either! When I joined they gave me a book and advised me to read it and it would inform me how to be a good Kiwanian. The rules were that you pay your initiation fee, don't miss more than four meetings or make them up by going to some other club. All of the rules and regulations were handed to me to study, but unfortunately I did not study them too carefully. Anyway the rules were there and it was only a matter of external observation.

This external observation of rules is the way many people view Christianity. Present them a set of rules and regulations or a creed and tell them to do this or that and they will be Christians. If this is so, Christianity has nothing of any significance whatever to offer the world. If, as opposed to this approach (which is Judaism), people recognize that they cannot successfully keep the rules because it is not in man to do so, then they must find a subjective experience by divine grace. These honest folks will then find life and hope.

God does something real in salvation. It is not man subscribing to the Ten Commandments or anything else. It is no longer a matter of mere religion with a set of regulations and rules. It is a new life in us with a heart-beating throb, with a living reality that pulsates to flow out of us in action. But it is difficult for many to see.

Whoever heard of a mother, having given birth to a baby, giving it the following kind of instructions: "Baby, if you will take a lot of air in through your nose or mouth it will go into your lungs and you will breathe; if you open up your eyelids, you will see; and baby, if you try you can wiggle your fingers." It is absurd! But this is precisely what too many people do, when they begin talking about being Christians. This only reveals that their thinking is objective. When we have to take one who has supposedly committed his life to Christ and instruct him on how to "wiggle" this and that according to our creed, it becomes as absurd as trying to teach a baby how to be human. It is the nature of a baby to be human. It will not grow up a dog, or a cat, or a monkey or any other kind of animal. It is equally true of the new nature of a genuinely regenerated person.

Paul, in I Corinthians, chapter 2, and verse 16, says, "For who has known the mind of the Lord, that he may give the Lord some kind of instruction?" But he quickly adds, "We *have* the mind of the Lord." Let us remember this.

In I John, chapter 3 verse 9, John continues to use the figure of the new birth, "Whosoever is born of God does not practice (the same) sin (continually), for God's seed remains in him." The word for "seed," in the Greek, is "sperma." It is the same concept as natural procreation. Whoever is born of God has the "sperm" of God. This is what makes Christianity distinctive from other religions. It is a subjective experience. The seed of God is implanted by grace through the Holy Spirit with all the propensities thereof.

Peter in his second letter, chapter 1, verse 4, says, "That ye may become partakers of the divine nature."

If all we can say to the world is that we are Christians because we joined the church, then we are not one bit different from any other organization except that we are labelled church as opposed to Kiwanis Club. But if, in fact, through our faith in Jesus Christ, God has touched our souls and the "sperma" of God has been planted in us, then our souls are now made alive toward God in an intimate, organic fellowship and relationship.

Let us take John's concept a little farther because it is the wonder of Christianity. This is the miracle that has been missing for so many.

When the seed of a man and the seed of a woman come together, each gives its chromosomes and consequent genetic structure to the new embryo. The new life will carry genetic characteristics of parents and grandparents for generations back. It will carry propensities as well as physical characteristics. The family traits and characteristics are there. It is in the very nature of them. It is also true that God, in causing us to be born again by faith in Jesus Christ, has, in fact, imparted to us spiritually, an equally real characteristic of Himself. It is a re-creation. It is a new birth.

Paul says in Colossians that the new birth re-establishes in us the image of God that sin had destroyed. This is where the root of the argument of works and faith really lies. The people who are arguing for what we must do, completely miss this point in their thinking. There is nothing we can do, either before or after we are saved that will make us complete.

Our relationship with God is one that comes from a spiritual nature created by a spiritual act. It does not mean that, for example, when a child is born, he will automatically do everything his parents want him to do, nor does it mean that children are always a good reflection of their parents.

We had better recognize this, or we shall be in trouble.

It is equally true, in the realm of the Spirit, that we can be implanted by God's Holy Spirit in a new relationship and still be a baby in Christ with all that that means. We don't become gods when we become Christians.

Babies can be the most selfish creatures in the world. The Bible says we are "born in sin and shapen in iniquity." People who do not believe this have never raised a child or else are totally blind to their child's faults.

Babies; what a bundle of unrelatedness; what a bundle of irrelevancy. They do not know how to do anything properly. Messed up diapers, messed up carpets, clothes, sloppy eating, yet we keep loving those little creatures. We know that some day, with the proper training we can bring out the best in them. Hopefully, they will improve. At least until they are teenagers. We have a friend in Miami who has two teenagers and he says the only way God could answer his prayer about his teenagers is that they should be buried when they are 13 and raised again when they are 20. It is not quite that bad!

We are trying to get over the message that an infant human may not be all that we want him to be, but by nature, he has all the ingredients to produce maturity. The baby does not receive a second blessing or become a second kind of human when he is an adolescent. Everything that we are, is what we had when we were born. All the potential of adulthood and maturity is in the baby. It needs only nurture, care and development. Similarly, everything that a believer needs in relationship to God is complete when he is regenerated. We need nothing else by nature. To say otherwise is to insult the concept of God in the New Testament.

I'M HUMAN—THANK GOD

One of the reasons we have recently seen so much seeking after second works of grace, second blessings, and all the other doctrines of works, is the carnality of our nature. We want salvation to be something we know we are doing. We are not content to say we are saved by grace alone because we are simply not so sure. We are preoccupied with trying to prove to others that we are.

We are not denying that there is Christian responsibility of action. There is. We are saying that when we became Christians God gave us, in the Holy Spirit, everything He knows to give us to become his child. He also took the care to put us in a family of people who are his children. This is the reason for the local church. This is why it was established. It was not established as an organization for statistical accomplishment. Whoever heard of a baby being born and being left on a doorstep, except by somebody who was deranged? Surely, we cannot say that of God!

When the Bible speaks of the church, some feel that it does not mean the local church, but rather the total body of Christ. This is like saying to a baby, "we will leave you on the sidewalk, for you are in the whole family of people in the world." The world of people will take good care of it, won't they? We do not give up a life like this. So the New Testament reports that daily, as people came to know Christ, they were baptized and added to the local church.

There the family of God is at different stages of spiritual development like any human family. The new arrivals will learn in the ordinary give and take, by the instruction of the divine Word and by the Holy Spirit in the fellowship of believers. They will learn to grow in grace and in the knowledge of the Lord. Everything that God has for them in Christ may develop in them. Their mind will be the renewing factor. They take in the things they receive which will be confirmed by the subjective experience and assimilated into the new person. This places an awesome responsibility on the local church, its fellowship and programs.

There is no magic in Christian growth and development. We do not have to find a secret place or go to the mountains; nor do we have to wait until we hear a clap of thunder or see a flash of lightning. There is absolutely no necessity for mysticism. Christian growth is a spontaneous and practical experience and development just as natural growth and development. If we renew our minds guarding everything that comes into them, being our own censors under the Holy Spirit, this will make our lives constructive and wholesome. What we think is what we are. If we do this our lives will be transformed.

What does the word "transformed" mean? It means, we are the same person yet different. How is that for a paradox? The Greek word used in this context for transformed is transliterated into English as metamorphosis.

I suppose the best example of metamorphosis is the caterpillar. The caterpillar goes into a cocoon like a worm, and it comes out a butterfly. It is the same as it went in, in many respects. It is the same organism, and yet it comes out with a wholly different disposition. It is the same, yet it is different! Here is one of the things Christians find difficult to understand. They think that to become a Christian is to become dehumanized. Can I dare say it to illustrate my point? It is as if the caterpillar were to say when it enters the cocoon, "I'm going to be decaterpillarized." It is not! It is still there. It moves into a higher, better, more sophisticated and more beautiful form.

So Paul says, in effect, "by the renewing of your mind, and the inner experience of the Holy Spirit, you as believers, while you are yet in your humanity will be experiencing a metamorphosis." There will be the same you but you will take on higher, more beautiful, more significant characteristics.

The same Greek word is used in Matthew 17, but is there translated, transfigured. Jesus was transfigured, before Peter, James and John. Here is another analogy for us. What happened to him when he was transfigured? He radiated the glory of heaven, but not in an unreal sense. He was talking with Moses and Elijah who were historical figures.

Have you ever thought of the Mount of Transfiguration in the context of God's over-all purpose for the world? What He had been doing at one point in history through Moses, and the prophets, He is, in these last days, doing through Jesus. On the Mount of Transfiguration we have, as it were, God's three quarterbacks. They are together discussing and comparing the plays of all history, and their respective parts.

The Transfiguration ties in the generations past with the present and brings hope to the future. We see in it the over-all purpose of God in the world.

Thus the Transfiguration of Jesus is not an experience which is merely mystical and unreal, but a means by which we can see the reality of the world that continues unseen. The Transfiguration assures us the saints are very much alive and aware. They are evidently still intensely interested in the world.

By renewing our minds we enter into a metamorphosis. Metamorphosis is a slow change. It is not an instantaneous thing. It is a process. John says it beautifully, "It doth not yet appear what we shall be, but we know that, when he shall appear, we shall be like him for we shall see him as he is." It will not be until he appears that we shall appear as we are to appear. We know we are in the process of change, but we also know we are born of God. Because we know this, we ought to do everything that is spiritually practical to improve our growth and development, in partnership with God, the Holy Spirit.

CHAPTER 11

Transformation to Non-conformity

One of the great difficulties we have as Christians is our tendency to be legalistic. We would like to be told what to do. We have been contending that the heartbeat of Christianity is not showing people how to do it, but receiving God's power. Religions show us how to do it but do not impart any capability. The Old Testament is mere religion. It is objective to the person. It is external. It failed, not because it was not good, as Paul has noted and as Jesus affirmed, but simply because humans did not have the capability of fulfilling the law. It is not in our capacity to do it. James points out very clearly that we may boast about keeping nine of the Ten Commandments but if we break one we have broken them all. And so legalism becomes a frustration to us. To almost win is to lose.

We were ice hockey fans when we lived in Canada and we used to get very annoyed when it was reported that the Montreal Canadians were defeated 1-0. I mean, one point to nothing! That did not seem to constitute a defeat. If they had said 10-0, we could have understood using the word "defeat." But just one little point.

I'M HUMAN—THANK GOD

But the real significance is that whether we are defeated by one point or ten points, we are defeated! This is the principle of any kind of legalism, of any kind of external religious form. It is a source of utmost frustration because it is not subjective, but external, objective to us.

We have seen how transformation is a subjective experience; something that has happened within us which gives us capabilities to be spiritual.

The word "transformed" could give us all kinds of excuses to become religiously abstract, head-in-the-cloud types. We have met them. They assume an air of being above and beyond the common run of men. This is always the sure sign of a weak Christian.

Have you noticed this in the Bible that the nearer a man comes to God, the less aware he is of the fact? Remember how Job put it, "I have seen Jehovah, and I think I'm just about the greatest man around." That was not the reaction that came from him at all! He says, "I have seen the Lord and I abhor myself." The closer we come to the holiness of God, the more conscious we become of our total inability to be holy as he is holy. The nearer we come to God, the less aware we are of our spirituality.

Transformation is a practical thing. It is a vital thing.

As we have already observed in the figure of the new birth, a baby has something intrinsic to itself by nature. If we are genuinely born of the Spirit of God, we will likewise begin to do spiritual things because we are spiritual by the work of grace. We do not react because someone gives us a lecture on how to do it but because it is the nature of us to do it. So much for the word "transformed."

TRANSFORMATION TO NON-CONFORMITY

The next word of importance in Romans 12:2 is this word "conformed." Strangely enough in II Corinthians 11, verses 13-15, the same word is used but translated "transformed." This is not the same Greek word we looked at in the last chapter. The word for conformed is compounded from the word "schematic." The II Corinthian reference uses it in its negative sense but is highly informative for our purpose. It reads: "For such are false apostles, deceitful workers, transforming themselves into apostles of Christ. And no marvel, for Satan himself is transformed into an angel of light." Transliterated the word for "transformed" in this context is our word, "schematic," as in schematic drawing. The word implies not something that we do by nature, but something that we are by copying. It is not intrinsically ours. It is the idea that we are following a schematic drawing prepared by another or of something we have observed outside of ourselves. It is not intrinsic to us.

Satan is not a new creation nor are his followers, but they can come to be "Angels of Light" by this schematic principle. They can copy the characteristics of a Spirit-filled life.

The reason the scripture has used two different words is very important, because, in the one case it is simply a "copying of" and in the other it is a "possession of." We have millions of professing Christians who copy the Christian ethic. They believe this is Christianity but they are not possessors of a new life through faith in Jesus Christ. It is distinctly possible, then, to copy Christian ethics without being a Christian. We can endeavor to copy the ethic of Jesus yet never know anything about him spiritually. This is the distinctive meaning of these two words.

Believers must not "schematic" their new lives after that of the unregenerate world. The believer has a changed life by the power of God, by an internal experience. If he is to be like the world, he will, therefore, have to fashion his life by copying the schematic of the unregenerate. He will really be going against himself. It is against his new nature. His new nature will seek to live out the life of the Spirit. In other words, this scripture says that, for the truly regenerated Christian, being worldly is something he has to work at. It will be a return to a life untouched by saving grace.

If we allow the Spirit of God who is in us to work through us, being spiritual is normal. It is high time we put Christianity in these terms because we have too often left it on the basis of a schematic.

To be of the world the believer in effect has to willfully determine to go contrary to the new nature within him. This is why he is unhappy while he is doing it because it is contrary to his new self. Here is his frustration.

I often have young Christians inquire why, since they have become Christians, life seems to be more difficult than it was before. We sometimes hear it said that life is easier when men come to Christ, but don't ever believe it. There is no proof of this either in experience or in the Bible.

Have you ever tried going against the crowd? I tried it one Christmas when I was in a real hurry to get out of a building when it seemed everyone else was coming in. When we become Christians this is where the problem arises because we are going in the opposite spiritual direction from the rest of the crowd in the way we live. This is nothing to get upset about.

Tension is necessary for spiritual growth. Swimming is a tension between the swimmer and gravity which would pull him to the bottom of the pool. If we don't react properly to the tension by counteracting gravity, we will go to the bottom. But look at the fun we get out of that tension! In this sense we speak of tension in spiritual things. It can become a joy for we have the capability in Christ to overcome the world, the flesh and the devil. Tension is not to be rejected.

If we have renewed our minds and if we have, in fact, been transformed and are in this metamorphosis in which God is changing our lives, then we will know that we cannot copy the spirit and attitude of the world and feel at peace within.

"Be not conformed to the world." What do you mean by the term "world"? We have heard many definitions of what this means. When I was growing up in Scotland it meant all kinds of humorous things. It meant, for example, in our particular group, that women did not go to the beauty parlor. Getting one's hair waved was very worldly. If a woman wore earrings, she was worldly. The girls and women were not allowed to live by the fashions, but by the Board of Deacons! We even had one board which prescribed the length skirts should be. Going to the movies was worldliness. Sunday School teachers were not allowed to use cosmetics. The girls got around this nicely. They did not wear cosmetics to Sunday School, but they went out between Sunday School and church and put them on. There were all kinds of ways to get around the problem. This is always the way with legalism. Legalists eventually become like the scribes and Pharisees of the New Testament and find all kinds of ways to by-pass the laws.

When we crossed over to England, we discovered that we were in a new world. We could go to the football games in England. Our group opposed our going to the games in Scotland. But they had other restrictions with which I shall not weary you.

Then, of course, when one goes on over to the Continent, the legalistic believers have yet another set of rules. It is much easier to live on the Continent.

When we came to Canada it was even a little easier to live. When we went into the northern part of the United States it was easier still. Now that we are in the South, we are completely liberated!

All of this is the way people try to interpret the word "worldly." It reminds us of the chameleon. Chameleons are the little creatures who change their color to suit their background. My wife and I finally got to the place where we experienced so many different forms of legalism that we decided that wherever we were we would change our background to suit the group with which we were working.

Do you know what killed the chameleon? Somebody put it on a piece of Scottish plaid and it died in the attempt. This is precisely what we get with legalism. We can get ourselves so utterly, totally and completely confused, that we do not even know where we are. If this is how you interpret the word "worldly" then you have my sympathy, because you have not learned the truth of the verse that says, "whom the Son sets free is free indeed."

TRANSFORMATION TO NON-CONFORMITY

What is this word that is used here for "world?" First of all, the word has little to do with people at all. It is not the word "cosmos" that is sometimes translated "world." The word is "aeon." It means the spirit that is of the unregenerate age. It is a spirit. If we were trying to define the word in modern terms, it would be what the social psychologist would call a universal psychology. It is that! It is the universal driving motivation of the crowd who know nothing about redeeming grace nor the indwelling power of the Holy Spirit. Paul therefore contrasts the spirit of the age with Spirit of God in the believer.

The spirit of the world is that which motivates the mass of people who have not been regenerated by Christ, while that which motivates the believer is the Holy Spirit. If you want to know what worldliness is in the biblical sense, it is that which negates the actions of the Holy Spirit. This is a lot more sophisticated than legalism.

We have experienced difficulty in church conferences where we have made this emphasis, because people find it more comfortable to follow the legalistic line. They prefer to think that rules make good Christians. This kind of people seldom gets down to the real fruits of the Spirit. For one thing they are much more difficult to perform.

It is much more difficult for example to love with "agape" love which is the first of the fruits of the Spirit, than to stop smoking. In the measure that we as believers do not allow the Holy Spirit to live through us in "agape" love, in that measure we are worldly. This puts a lot of us into the place of being worldly.

It is so difficult to have "agape" love. It requires

such submission! We prefer to excuse ourselves from loving certain kinds of people, but in the New Testament we do not have an option whom we should love. Jesus came into this world by one motivating factor—"God so loved the world." This is "agape" love. "Agape" belongs distinctively to God and is distinctively a New Testament experience under the Holy Spirit. "Agape" gives us no options. We cannot choose the kind of people we shall love, anymore than God. He gives the full effect of all His love to the world. They do not all receive it, and they do not all respond to it, but He gives it to them.

When Jesus said to us, "Go ye into all the world," he was simply passing on the responsibility that God, the Father, has given to Him as a Son to reveal "agape" to all mankind. He passed the responsibility on to us and sent us out to give it to the world. But we cannot give it to the world until we have it.

John in his first letter said, "If a man says that he loves God (that is "agape") and hates his brother he is a liar and the truth is not in him." He has never been born again. He has perhaps tried to follow the schema of Christianity, but he has not had the experience of it in the inner parts of his life.

Don't let us forget the other evidences of the Spirit's life in us. God does other things besides love, you know.

Joy is the next of them. God's Spirit in us will produce spiritual exhilaration. Enthusiasm and zeal are but an expression of happiness. Happiness is God's gift. It is something that comes through the Holy Spirit. The measure in which we lose our sense of joy in living, joy of being, we allow ourselves to take on the form of a world that is anything but joyful. The world is pleasure-ridden, but not joyful. When Christians are constantly complaining about one thing or another and are irksome, all they are doing is hanging out their emotional shingle and saying, "I am out of fellowship with the Lord." It is not very smart to give oneself away like that.

Then there is peace. This word is used in so many different ways today, but here it is the "peace of God that passeth understanding." It is not necessarily the absence of outside conflict because if we are believers we are going to have that in the world.

I once saw peace beautifully illustrated at Niagara Falls when we first arrived from Scotland. We went to the Falls and came over to the American side. At that time we were too poor to afford to go on the Maid of the Mist, the little boat that takes tourists around the Falls, so we just looked at others going down. As we stood and watched them, our ears were almost deafened with the sound of the falls crashing over the precipice. The mist from the falls comes like a big cloud over the area. As we watched the people going down into the boat with their raincoats on, we noticed a tree growing out of the side of the precipice. There were very few of them on that rocky precipice at the side of the falls. There, perched on the end of the tree, was a bird. We could not hear if there was singing. We did notice that now and again his beak opened and we came to the con-clusion that he was trying to be heard over the noise and the din. As I looked at that little bird, I said to my wife, "I'm going to use that from now on as an illustration of what the New Testament means by peace." With all the noise, commotion, din, power and strength all around it, that little creature could care less. It was in the midst of it all in complete tranquility. This is the peace that God gives. The world cannot give it.

Even though Calvary is all around Jesus, there is peace in his soul. "My peace I give unto you, not as the world gives." He gives us peace, so that in the midst of the tensions, we can live with ourselves. This is mental health at its ultimate! If you are one of those Christians who is always restless, discontented, torn asunder, full of strife and argument, let me tell you it is not because you have a lot of convictions but rather because you are lacking in conviction. The confused, crotchety, contentious believer is simply displaying his lack of commitment to God and the Holy Spirit.

When our children were growing up and someone was contentious, instead of barking at each other, we would say "your worldliness is showing." That changed us faster than a good argument! If I were driving the car in traffic and another driver irritated me and I was about to show him how I felt about it, then I would hear voices piping out the back, "Daddy, your worldliness is showing."

The fruits of the Spirit are much more significant than whether we smoke, or whatever is the going legalism now. These things are relatively unimportant in relation to higher spiritual values. This is what will make the world take notice that we have been with God. With this they will be attracted.

The best-selling books are those purporting to help people live. Christians have never successfully gotten over to the world the real source of contented living.

TRANSFORMATION TO NON-CONFORMITY

The reason is because the world has not seen too much of this kind of living in those who claim to know it. Now there is a tragedy! Before we verbalize our witnessing we must concentrate more in getting the experience predominant in our own lives.

I had an encounter with some young Christians at the University of Miami not too long ago. I was suggesting that it was time to quit talking so much about witnessing and go on the premise of living the Christian life. One of them shot back with "What are you going to do with the verse that says, 'give a reason for the hope that is within you'?" I replied that there was no such verse in the Bible. Nearly all of them turned quickly to their Bibles to show me how wrong I was! This is not what the verse says at all. This is only part of the verse. The verse says, ". . . and be ready always to give an answer to every man that asketh a reason for the hope etc." Some of us simply do not have the good manners to wait until we are asked. Do you know why? Because we are afraid no one is ever going to ask us. And we are right. If people do not ask us for the reason for the hope that is within us it is because they do not see anything worth inquiring about. Excuse me, I did not mean to be so blunt, but that is what the verse says.

We may know Christ, but Christianity and church will become a colossal bore and a burden to us if we are only half-living it. Believe me, it will. But if we give this new life a chance to work through us, we shall experience the thrill of the happy life. This is what it means by "working out our salvation." We cannot work it out until it has been wrought in us and it is only wrought in us by the Holy Spirit in the new birth. So, try it!

I'M HUMAN—THANK GOD

Men, shock your wives by being real good fellows. Be real nice around the house. Young people, shock your mother, make your bed in the morning. When you come home from school, tell her you feel this is the way Christ would have you do things from now on. Instead of walking off and leaving your responsibilities to someone else, let your "agape" for your Mom come through. Have a try at it. It is amazing what it does. We can change a home; we can change our society; we can change our church. People like this are non-conformists in the sense of our society.

This is really the thing called revival. Real revival is when Christians become what God means them to be. When this day comes we will not be able to contain the crowds, for people will come to see this thing that has come to pass. They will ask us, "what in the world happened?" Then we will be able to give reasons that are meaningful and they will listen to our reasons because they will want what we have. This is the basis for all genuine evangelism. Anything else is contrived.

CHAPTER 12

God Needs Bodies
as Well as Souls

In the New Testament there is a consistent emphasis on the body of the believer. "I beseech you therefore brethren by the mercies of God, that ye present your bodies a living sacrifice, holy, acceptable unto God, which is your reasonable service." "Know ye not that your body is the temple of the Holy Spirit."

We might wonder what is really the significance of verses such as these. At the very heart of it there is a different and necessary concept of evangelism involved. As I have already indicated we have come through a time in which evangelism has been equated with a professional evangelist, a professional preacher, or a certain kind of preaching, a certain kind of message. I believe that these are only a very tiny part of what the New Testament means by evangelism. I think, too, that the Church has failed to meet the needs of the world as rapidly as it ought because believers have had a restricted concept of evangelism. Evangelism, in the New Testament, is the total activity of all believers at any given moment of any day through their personal experiences. When we put evangelism in these terms, it takes it out of the pulpit and the sanctuary, and places it wherever there is a believer.

I'M HUMAN—THANK GOD

The concept of the priesthood of the believer contains the thought of evangelism. The believer, being a priest, does not, by the way, make him a pastor. We have had too much emphasis recently on the priesthood of the believer that has downgraded the office of the pastor. This is totally unbiblical. A priest's function is to intercede, a priest's function is to come between, a priest's function is to worship and lead in worship toward God. That is not, primarily, a pastoral function. We must distinguish between the doctrine of the priesthood of the believer which gives each one the right to intercede with God on behalf of others and the right to be a personal center of worship, and the office of Pastor.

Priesthood does not give each believer the equivalent of the ministry of the divinely appointed office of pastor and teacher within the body of believers. To downgrade the pastoral office in order to proclaim the priesthood of the believer is untheological and unscriptural, but it has happened too often in many of the lay movements around today.

Each believer has to become a "God-center," not only in the pew, or when we kneel to pray, or open a Bible, but with every heartbeat of life. Our total life is the area of evangelism. You may not necessarily talk about Jesus because true evangelism is not merely *verbalizing* the gospel. It is BEING the gospel. And being the gospel will be you, whatever you are doing, wherever you are. This is why we are all evangelists.

Several years ago, I was invited to lead the Air Force chaplains of the Southwest Command in their annual retreat. The Chief Chaplain called me and asked if I would do this, and I replied that I would be happy to come and share with the chaplains. About a week later, he called back and asked if I had decided on a subject. I told him my subject would be "The Sacrament of Service." There was a hush at the other end of the telephone, and I confess I expected it because the good Colonel was a Southern Baptist. When he spoke, he said, "McMillan, you are a Baptist, aren't you?" I replied in the affirmative. "You did say your subject was the 'Sacrament of Christian Service'?" I said, "Yes." He said, "Well, how in the world does a Baptist ever talk about sacraments?" I replied, "Well, why don't you wait and find out?"

There are some beautiful words that we have yielded up to what we today call the sacramentalists, such as the Roman Catholics and Episcopalians. This word "sacrament" is one such word which in its original use was a very important word, in my mind, for what I understand about the believers' body and evangelism.

Let us look at the word "sacrament," carefully. Augustine defined it as "a visible sign of an invisible grace." Calvin declared it to be "an external sign by which the Lord seals on our conscience his promise of good-will toward us in order to sustain us in the witness of our faith so that we in our turn can testify our piety toward him." Calvin said there had to be a rule to identify a sacrament. Calvin's rule was, "There must be a promise of God, and a command of the Lord, and the word of God which promises in the external, visible sign the presence of the Holy Spirit." What these two men said, we can accept. God uses tangible, visible means to communicate himself to the world. This is the old concept of sacrament.

I'M HUMAN—THANK GOD

We reject the later idea that the visible sign itself becomes divine. It never did mean this originally. This is what sacramentalists have made of it who, for example, believe there is something intrinsic to the bread and the wine in communion which makes them divine. We cannot believe this. We do believe, however, that God of necessity has to use visible, tangible, physical, sensible, humanly comprehensible means to communicate himself. The reason he has to do so is because God is spirit.

The Authorized Version quotes Jesus as saying, "God is a Spirit." In the original the indefinite article is not justified. God is not a Spirit among other spirits. The Greek makes it clear, God is Spirit, and if there are any other spirits they had to be created by God. God is distinctively unique.

The Westminster Confession says, "God is spirit having no bodily parts." Now there is a problem! It is the problem of divine communication. How can God, Eternal Spirit, who has no bodily parts, communicate with us who primarily relate through our bodily and physical senses? How can God a "Spirit, eternal, invisible, immortal" to quote the Westminster catechism, communicate with us who primarily comprehend by what we see, touch, hear and smell etc. This is a major problem.

God who is Spirit, eternal, immortal, invisible and infinite thinks and moves in a totally different plane from us. How can He communicate so that we restricted humans can begin to know him? This is the ultimate demand of the Incarnation. It makes divine communication complete.

GOD NEEDS BODIES AS WELL AS SOULS

Let me try to illustrate the problem of divine human communication. Suppose I had a jug of water and a smaller glass. The jug of water would be like infinity. If I try to transfer all the water from the jug to the glass, it cannot be done. There is no way to do it. Here is the problem of God's communication with us. I realize God's infinity is not quantitative but qualitative but the illustration conveys an idea. There is no point, God being who He is and we who we are, at which we shall ever know the fullness and wonder of the glory in Him.

We can never be in danger of asking too much of God since there is no possibility of humans, even in their fondest dreams, exhausting either his ability or power. So never refrain from expecting great things from God. When we say great things from God, we mean the greatest things you can imagine. Barth has a statement which is true, that "when we have come to man's furthermost point, we are at God's beginning." Isn't that thrilling? Do you get excited about it?

The next wonder is that God wants to communicate with us. In order to do so He reaches out of his infinitude and communicates with us in visible means we are capable of comprehending.

Remember how Moses saw the burning bush? That was God using a visible means to communicate himself. Sometimes people say Christians should not engage in promotion. We could not begin to come close to the kind of promotion God goes for. Whoever announced a birth and sent a whole choir of angels to sing about it? Whoever commissioned a star to go through the sky? Makes Madison Avenue look cheap, doesn't it? In Moses' case, God used a visible thing, the burning bush, and as it is burned, Moses went aside to see because the curious part was that it was not being consumed. At that moment, God communicated a mystery of himself. He stopped the man, surprised the man, made the man inquisitive and now He will talk to him. "Take off the shoes from off thy feet for the ground on which thou standest is holy ground." And Moses, through this visible means, entered into communication with the invisible God.

The people of Israel needed to know God was with them. In those days they had a disadvantage which we do not possess. They were in the process of receiving the revelation. We have it! So we no longer need a pillar of fire by night nor a pillar of cloud by day. It is no longer necessary. But these people were in the process of receiving the revelation of God which became part of the divine written record. We, for our part, now have the divine written record and their witness to satisfy us. These pillars of cloud and of fire were visible means by which through their senses, they knew God was communicating. God was saying, "go" or "stop" by these signs as they journeyed through the wilderness.

God also gave Israel the Tabernacle. Almost every part of the visible structure of the Tabernacle conveyed a spiritual message. The sacrifices of the Old Testament were also visible means of communicating the invisible grace and ministry of God. A learning people needed these materialized communications, and so we see them throughout the Old Testament.

When we come to the New Testament, we see the ultimate. We confront God's last Word. This is the declaration of Hebrews, chapter 1 and verse 1, "God, who at sundry times and in divers manners spake in time past unto the fathers by the prophets, hath in these last days spoken unto us by his Son, Jesus Christ." Jesus, in the Incarnation, is God's last Word. But it is a visible word. It is a living Word, as opposed to the written word. It is God become flesh and dwelling among us.

In Jesus Christ who is the express image of God, we can look and learn dimensions of God in love and grace we could not discover in any other way. The Incarnation is the ultimate of divine revelation. It was essential that God give such a revelation if we were to know him in any sense of human understanding. And so, once again, the visible communicates the invisible.

When Jesus left the world, he left visible and significant witnesses that are important. In most churches if the gospel is not proclaimed verbally, there are visible evidences of the total message of the gospel left by the will and the word of God in the ordinances. So long as there is a visible communion table, and so long as there is a visible baptistry, there is a whole gospel. In the one we have the message of the sacrificial atonement of the blood of Jesus Christ shed for the remission of sins; in the other, the baptistry, we have the death, burial, and resurrection of Christ portrayed. These are two continuing visible means of communicating God. But what about those who do not know the Lord? What is God doing visible for them? It is not the bricks and mortar of a church on the corner that is the communication for them.

The body of the individual believer becomes the scriptural, physical, visible communicator of the grace of God to the world. This is why the believer's body is important. God has no other hands, He has no other lips to speak. He has no other body in which he now lives except the believer. And so the apostle says, "Christ in me." This has to be the most awesome statement of the New Testament, "Christ in me, the hope of glory."

What is the glory of God? Some will talk about the Shekinah glory of the Old Testament; a light that shines. But where is it now to be seen? The glory of God is the sum total of his manifested attributes. "Christ in me" is the hope of the divine attributes being communicated. The fruits of the Spirit, being manifested in the believer's body are divine attributes. We should glorify God by these visible, tangible, sensible, understandable means that ought to be observable in us. When this happens, we have truly communicated God in Christ. Most believers have never realized this. This is evangelism in true perspective.

Why has this not been more carefully propagated? We have been taught and preached at on how to get saved in order to get ready to die. In almost every sermon we were told to prepare for eternity. Christianity in my early life—and it is true in most evangelistic churches—was a means of getting ready to check out of this world. Very few took time out to say that it is of utmost importance to God that, instead of living to die, we die to live.

Our bodies, with their talents, abilities, mind, physical prowess, become, in a beautiful way, a tangible communication of God who is in us. Obviously this does not mean walking around with the biggest Bible we can get. That is artificial. In any case, the Bible tells us that we are far better when we walk around to hide his word in our hearts so we might not sin against Him. It is much more important in there than carrying it outside.

Take, for example, the ministry of healing commanded in the great commission. Is there a difference between this and the healing practice of doctors who are not Christians? Here is another reason why the believer's body is important. What believers do may be very similar to what an unbeliever does at any given moment, but how we do it should make it a divine communication. Here also is the problem of a lopsided emphasis of the so-called social gospel. We do not have to be Christian to do the right thing, socially. What we do should have a totally different motivation from non-Christians even if they are engaged in the same kind of work.

There should be a difference between Christian counseling and non-Christian counseling for example. A non-Christian counselor and a Christian counselor may use the same instruments in their work, but there should be a difference in the outcome of that work. There should be a communication of God in Christ. It may not necessarily be verbalized but it should be noticeable.

If I am thirsty, an atheist could give me a cup of water. That would be no more than humanitarian. But the scripture enjoins a believer to give "a cup of cold water in the name of the Lord." The phrase "the name of the Lord" implies motivation by the person of Jesus Christ in me. I should not only give a cup of cold water (humanitarian), but I should also somehow communicate Jesus Christ to the recipient. He should feel that my act is Christ oriented.

This is the idea behind the word "sacrament" as we are using it. It is a visible sign of divine activity. Jesus caught it. He fed the five thousand, he felt their need, he felt their hunger, he felt that they were tired, he felt they were exhausted, and he felt and accepted the social responsibility for them. He also translated the feast into divine communication. The next day, however, he did not. They were still there. They followed him to the other side of the lake and when he arrived he talked to them and said, in effect, "Why have you come today? Because yesterday I fed you? You are here today, not because you want me nor because you need me, but in order to see another miracle and receive another social hand-out." And he did not perform the miracle for them that day.

There is an important distinction here. We Christians can glorify God because his Spirit is living in us and our body, therefore, becomes the temple of the Holy Spirit. We have in fact become the visible communicators of the living Christ in our society. We are Christ centered. There should be as many Christ centers in our community as there are believers in fellowship with God. Here is saturation evangelism!

The Christian doctor, in a very real sense, can say, "I am practicing in the name of Christ." It is the work of the Holy Spirit to translate this into a divine communication. It is our responsibility to do it in the person of Christ.

Can you imagine what would happen in the world if every Christian, some at school, some in the banks, some professors, some attorneys, some in the Legislature, some home-making, would glorify God in their bodies? What a manifestation of God would enter the community! I hope that you will realize this significance of your body. Our bodies are different from an unbeliever's because ours are indwelt by the Spirit of God. God wants to work through us his grace and his purpose in divine communication.

CHAPTER 13

Prayer

Prayer is a very important subject for us to consider as we seek a practical and intelligent expression of our faith. As a young Christian I was always greatly disturbed about the subject for the connotation of prayer invariably meant going somewhere and getting down on your knees and uttering words. It usually also meant, in those early days of Christian experience, asking God for all kinds of things related to daily living. I did learn very early that if any subject was important enough for me to think about, it was important enough to pray about. I had no inhibitions about this matter and for that reason I was able to pray about every conceivable thing that happened or could happen in my life.

There came a great problem however and it was that the pressure of day-to-day activities prevented me experiencing what I had read about great saints who supposedly spent multiplied hours in this kind of prayer. It seemed a very practical question how they had the time and who paid them while they were doing all this particular kind of praying. It seemed to me that in order to be this kind of saint one would have to go to a monastery where someone was paying the bills so that you could spend the necessary time in this kind of exercise which spiritually gave you an edge in sainthood.

I'M HUMAN—THANK GOD

There was also the problem that the Bible used phrases such as "pray without ceasing. . ." This seemed to fit in with the latter concept if it were to mean getting alone and getting down on one's knees. It seemed to me that it was a highly impractical exercise and a contradiction of our Lord's injunctions to be busy, for example, multiplying our talents or to be hired in the marketplace as in one of the other parables and spending one's energy doing work for the Master.

All these points of view had a tendency to produce guilt feelings if in fact this is the true meaning of prayer. If this is not the true significance of prayer then perhaps we may find an answer that will relieve our souls of guilt feelings and help us enjoy our fellowship with the Lord.

Some of us can remember long, weary, yawning nights of prayer. As I recall them now they represented the ultimate of frustration caused by one or both of two attitudes. Either God was most reluctant unless we spent long hours coaxing and coercing Him to do things, or else it meant that those of us who spent long hours struggling with tiredness were afflicting our souls so that God would see our good works and reward us with whatever it was we were praying for. Then, too, there were others who felt that all of this was necessary because it wasn't easy to reach God because He was surrounded by demons and the devil. These had to be gotten by before one could reach the courts of heaven!

Of course there was yet another point of view that has already confronted us in these chapters of some who are so thoroughly convinced that God can only be reached if we embark upon a really physical punitive process.

What then is the real significance of Prayer? When Jesus gave instructions that we were to pray to the Father and in his name He gave us the fundamental meaning of prayer. It is, first of all, a family relationship. We are the children of God and He is our Father. It is, secondly, that our relationship to the Father is totally dependent upon the person of Jesus Christ.

The meaning of the phrase "in My name," is not, as some have indicated, that we present God a blank check with Jesus' signature on the bottom. Supposedly all we have to do is fill in the amount! This would be the height of parental folly, as humans, far less to be expected of the heavenly Parent. Any parent who hands his child a blank check telling him to fill in whatever he wants whenever he feels like it is headed for disaster and so is his child. It is foolishness. The phrase "in the name of Christ or of Jesus" means in his person. It is a phrase of relationship with the Father through Jesus Christ the Son. Prayer, by these terms, becomes, primarily, the attitude of the soul in relationship to God through faith in Jesus Christ.

We note, for example, concerning salvation that it says "God's Spirit witnesses with our spirit that we are born of God." This is the fundamental meaning of prayer. It is a relatedness of God's Spirit made possible through the work and ministry of Jesus Christ.

The attitude of your spirit to the eternal Spirit of God is the basic imperative of a prayer relationship that is meaningful. We can, however, have a very bad attitude towards God. In the Parable of the Talents, for example, the man who buried his talent used as an excuse that he knew his master was a despot and he feared him so, therefore, he buried his talent and did nothing with it. This is a very bad relationship. Nevertheless, there are many Christians who have such a relationship with God. Their attitude to Him is of exactly the same order because there is missing the basic ingredient of prayer which is an inter-communion between the Spirit of God and the believer.

As we look at the progress of revelation in the Bible we can also see the change in men's attitudes toward God.

In the opening chapters of the Bible, God is the awesome Creature behind the powers of nature. This is how Abraham came to know Him. While in Ur of the Chaldees he was worshiping the Sun-god. In the course of this nature-worship he heard the voice of the God behind nature.

When we come to Moses he inquires who God is and what kind of name he could give when he went to deliver the children of Israel from their bondage in Egypt. Here again the name in the Bible is significant of the person. God reveals to Moses the name Yahweh or Jehovah. This revelation is of a God who is more personal and who is related to time, events and the people of Israel. He is, in fact, the personal God of Israel. We must not despise this exclusiveness of God's personal relationship with Israel for out of it came the Law, the Prophets, the Covenant, the Temple, Worship, the Scriptures and, finally, Jesus Himself.

It is true that other nations and peoples in history have given us the names of gods but none like this One. The Greek gods for example are readily observed with a great deal of humor and some tragedy!

When we come to the New Testament the personal relationship with God reaches its ultimate when Jesus insists that we call him "Father."

When Jesus met the woman at the well she recognized the great debate as to where God was and to whom He belonged. She knew the Jews worshiped in the Temple at Jerusalem and the Samaritans worshiped in their own holy mountain. Jesus, however, exploded both points of view by announcing that the time was at hand when neither at Jerusalem nor in Samaria's mountains would God be worshiped. God was to be Father! He is Spirit and they that wish to have any relationship with Him will have it on a Spirit-to-spirit basis. Again Jesus removes the divine-human relationship from mere objectivity and places it in the heart of man.

Father, parenthood, children, family—all of these flood together in our thought processes. Here is a totally new attitude; an intimate relationship between God and man. Here there is family interaction and interest. There is mutuality of purpose. There is consultation. There is family security and responsibility. There is fatherly discipline and authority. There is paternal provision. There are family characteristics. The Father is in his children by divine act and the children are of their Father. There is an inevitable intertwining of the two by grace.

The Father! How Jesus loved the intimacy of that word and how that intimacy became indeed what is best known as prayer. There is no mere petition here! The attitude of the soul in the relationship is permanent because of salvation by grace. Even in rebellion the prodigal son knows his father whom he had spurned. It was prayer when he could utter within himself, "I will arise and go to my father." This is an attitude born of relationship. "I am not worthy. . ." is the expression of repentance for his rebellion against his family and his father. But the true relationship had not been altered! He knew his father! He also knew he could go home!

Prayer can be many things but it can be nothing unless it is a relationship and attitude of spirit. Now we can intelligently inquire how to pray without ceasing. The answer is, only if prayer is a relationship and an attitude of spirit. It is not merely a physical act on our knees nor is it necessarily linguistics.

Prayer is perpetual awareness of a relationship that affects our words, thoughts, and deeds. It is because of this persistent inner consultation in all of life's experiences that prayer becomes the blessing that it is. The relationship and attitude affects everything we do though we might never verbalize it in the way some people think of prayer.

Prayer is communion. But prayer is more than communion. It is many things more than communion. It is as we have seen a permanent relationship of the born again spirit of man with the Holy Spirit who is within. So, in a very real and significant sense, prayer is not necessarily lifting up our eyes toward heaven but is enjoyment and fellowship with the Holy Spirit.

Not only is the Holy Spirit within believers but also the Trinity. It must surely be obvious that we cannot have one without the other or else the doctrine of the trinity is meaningless. Paul can speak about "Christ in me the hope of glory" but he can also say "my life is hid with Christ in God." No matter which way we approach the subject we can see that it is an intertwining of our spirit with the eternal Spirit. I am in Him and He is in me. Can we dare believe this fantastic truth? We must, for this is truly the significant meaning of the Christian life.

Of course there are requests that we have to make known but it is universally agreed that this is only a paltry part of what we mean by prayer. In fact we, who are parents, know that it is the more immature of our children who are always asking for things! The more mature are restrictive in their petitions content with a relationship that has confidence in the father's sense of responsibility for his family.

There will be warm exchanges of gratitude and praise between God and us because of this attitude. This is another facet of prayer. It is not that God, or our earthly parents for that matter, needs our flattery to do more for us. God willingly accepts responsibility for his children. Our praise of spirit should be the filial expression of awe at the capability and responsibility of the Father's care for us in every area of our human need. For the Father's part, it is warmhearted to know that his children recognize his goodness towards them.

As I recall my childhood in Scotland I remember we had one room in our home we called the parlor. It was kept locked except on Sundays and on extremely important occasions. Among those occasions were times when my father and I needed to talk without anyone listening. These were moments of very serious encounter! It was a time when I needed a disciplined heart-to-heart talk in a secret place. I have to admit that some of those encounters were not happy ones but they were necessary! I always appreciated the fact that my father would take me quietly into the parlor and close the door so that the rest of the family were left outside. This is also true with God. Jesus instructs us to enter a room and pray to the Father in secret. These are times of special need. Dr. Paul Tournier in his book *Secrets* has adequately illustrated the necessity of this part of our relationship not only as human to human but also with God Himself. Every man is entitled to his own privacy!

The health-giving part of this kind of encounter relationship with the Heavenly Father cannot be overestimated. Getting the burden off our backs before the presence of our Father, secretly, knowing that he will evidence to us openly the effects of our encounter, is a relief for the soul.

We may call this kind of encounter confession. These times of personal encounter cannot be planned nor are they always necessary. The point of relationship and attitude does not demand long sieges to shake loose a reluctant Father. We must constantly keep before our minds that God gives to us by the measure of his grace and not by the measure of our self-affliction. There is no evidence whatsoever that God hands out special blessings for marathons of so-called prayer. These are more inclined to be pharisaical and biographical than spiritual. Our relationship with God is so intimate that God is never far from any one of us. To be separated from us is an impossibility for He is in us. Nor is there evidence that He is more attentive at midnight than at noon!

There will be times of vigil but these will be as spontaneous to arising situations as our relationship moment by moment with the Father. Any other type of vigil is the product of a contrived revivalism.

When the soul is heavy with spiritual malady it will specially seek the Father's presence. But even in this situation the soul will be deeply aware of a two-way spontaneity. It will be like sitting by the bedside of a sick loved-one until the fever breaks. There springs up a mutuality and a warm sense of relationship. This is a healthy one-to-one relationship that brings solace and assurance.

It will really be the healthy one who conducts the vigil! These moments of vigil, when they come, will find God, the "healthy" one, ministering to our malady until the spiritual fever breaks. In these cases the emotionally or spiritually sick believer has little choice in his condition but he has the permanent assurance of the presence of God within him. This is essential to the healing processes. So, in the depth of our spiritual relationship, this also is prayer, to know in a special way the Father is close by. We shall know it by the witness of his Spirit with ours.

In this relationship our spirit interacts with the Holy Spirit in normal day-to-day activities. Sometimes we will feel a burden for another member of the family or perhaps someone who is not in the family. This is called intercessory prayer. This kind of prayer is born by a deep sense of family relationship. We can see it illustrated by Mary at the wedding in Cana of Galilee when she said to Jesus "they have no wine." She knew and felt the need of her friends who were caught in a serious predicament. She used her holy relationship with Jesus to find a solution. Admittedly there was a very human error of attitude because she felt Jesus ought to do something because of her and not because of his own will.

I'M HUMAN—THANK GOD

Mary told the servants "whatsoever He tells you to do, do it." This is the confidence that is born of the divine human interaction and is an essential aspect of intercessory prayer. So we see that intercession is motivated by a spiritual relationship between God and us revealing mutual care for people.

We must remember that all of life's decisions are not momentous. Because of this our relationship and attitude will, on the whole, not be momentous. The overwhelming majority of hours of daily living will be free from the critical. But when a crisis comes critical action will be recognized in mutuality between us and God. It is our recognition that we are, in every aspect of living, in a perpetual relationship with God which is the significant purpose of prayer.

The early Christians sometimes testified to experiences of ecstasy in prayer. These were moments of very high emotional experience. We are confronted today with a movement among certain Christian groups to procure these ecstasies. Much of what is going on in the charismatic movement falls into this category. It is an endeavor to make these ecstatic experiences the spiritual norm. I cannot help but feel from observation that this is also a reflection of our days. The drug culture is also a reflection of our days. The common denominator to both these groups is escaping from the reality of day-to-day activities that have become boring. Each of these seek to produce ecstasy although by different means.

To believe that God has no relationship with us unless we are in perpetual emotional upheaval is perverse. There is such a thing as spiritual ecstasy. Some early writers spoke of the prayer relationship as spiritual intercourse. The reference is highly descriptive of intimacy and is, of course, taken from the marital relationship.

It must surely be obvious to any healthy-minded person that perpetual intercourse is not the norm to certify a happy marriage. This would be a perversion of the relationship! Any marriage built on this premise is infantile.

Ecstatic moments are meant to be unique, elevated and occasional. It is also true spiritually. The perpetual seeking after religious emotional highs is crass immaturity and spiritual perversion.

There will be times when in the presence of God we will have high moments of ecstatic expression. These will make us aware of the depth and intimacy of our relationship.

Prayer then is a permanent relationship of the Spirit of God with the spirit of the believer and will affect every moment of our living experience.

Robert M. McMillan was born in Glasgow, Scotland where he received his early education. He is a graduate of Skerry's College in Glasgow, the Scottish Bible Training Institute, Divinity School in London, England and Trinity College. He also completed graduate studies in Marriage and Family Counseling at St. Louis University. He has been an outstanding and revered leader in the Southern Baptist Convention for decades. In 1972 he was presented the Gold Medal by the DuPont Foundation, usually awarded to a research scientist. In 1973 McMillan was chosen Chaplain of the Florida State Senate. During his 64 years of ministry, McMillan has pastored churches in several countries including England, Canada and the United States. The last churches he served were two of the largest Baptist Churches in the Tallahassee, Florida area: the First Baptist Church of Tallahassee (15 years), and the Bradfordville First Baptist Church (7 years.) He is "Pastor Emeritus" for both churches. Dr. McMillan, now retired, resides in Tallahassee, Florida with his wife, Jeannie.